Jackson Hole Hikes

▲

Also by Rebecca Woods

Walking the Winds
A Hiking and Fishing Guide to
Wyoming's Wind River Range

Jackson Hole Hikes

Includes Grand Teton National Park &
Bridger-Teton and Targhee National Forests

by
Rebecca Woods

White Willow Publishing
Star Route 3272 • Jackson, Wyoming 83001

Acknowledgments

In addition to extensive field work, research for this guide was drawn from a large number of sources listed in the bibliography. Special thanks are extended to Fred Kingwill, information officer for Bridger-Teton National Forest; the staff at Teton County Library and Teton County Historical Center; and hiking companions Barbara Trachtenberg and Margie Reimers. The latter helped reconcile what was on the map with what was on the ground. What you see is not always what you get.

First Edition, 1993
Second Edition, 1996

©Copyright 1996 by Rebecca Woods
All rights reserved. No part of this book may be reproduced or transmitted in any form without written permission from the publisher, except for brief passages for articles or review. Address inquiries to: White Willow Publishing, Star Route 3272, Jackson, Wyoming, 83001.

CONTENTS

▲

Introduction 9
The Hikes:
GRAND TETON NATIONAL PARK
Introduction
1. Phelps Lake 19
2. Death Canyon/Static Peak 19
3. Taggart and Bradley lakes 22
4. Avalanche Canyon 25
5. Cottonwood Creek 26
6. Garnet Canyon 29
7. Lower Saddle 29
8. Amphitheater and Surprise lakes 33
9. Delta Lake 35
10. Jenny Lake 36
11. String Lake 36
12. Leigh and Bearpaw lakes 36

CASCADE CANYON
13. Hidden Falls and Inspiration Point 40
14. Forks of Cascade Canyon 40
15. Lake Solitude 40
16. Hurricane Pass/Alaska Basin 40
17. Hanging Canyon 46
18. Holly Lake and Paintbrush Divide 49
19. Schwabacher Landing 51
20. Hermitage Point 52
21. Lakeshore Trail 52
22. JLL to Colter Bay 55
23. Christian Pond 56
24. Emma Matilda Lake 58
25. Teton Crest Trail 61

5

THE WEST SLOPE

Introduction 65
26. Coal Creek and Taylor Mountain 67
27. Moose Creek 69
28. Game Creek and Housetop Mountain 70
29. Darby Canyon Wind and Ice Caves 72
SOUTH TETON CANYON
30. Devil's Stairs and Teton Canyon Shelf 75
31. Alaska Basin 75
32. Table Mountain 78
33. Green Lakes/South Leigh 80

TETON PASS

Introduction 82
34. Ridgetop Trail 84
35. Black Canyon 84
36. Old Pass Road 84
37. Ski Lake 87
38. Mail Cabin Creek 88
39. Burbank Creek 90
40. Oliver Peak 92

TETON VILLAGE

Introduction 95
41. Rendezvous Peak 97
42. Rock Springs Bowl 99
43. Tram to Marion Lake 101
44. Tram to Moose Lake 103
45. Granite Canyon 105

TETON WILDERNESS

Introduction 107
46. Box Creek Trail 109
47. Enos Lake 112
48. South Fork Falls 114
49. Holmes Cave 116
50. Arizona Creek 119
51. Huckleberry Ridge 121

TOGWOTEE PASS

Introduction 123
52. Jade Lakes 125
53. Upper Brooks and Rainbow Lake 126
54. Kisinger Lakes 128

GROS VENTRE RANGE

Introduction 131
55. Toppings Lakes 133
56. Gros Ventre Slide 135
57. Blue Miner Lake and Sheep Mountain 137
58. Red Hills 139
59. Shoal Falls 140
60. Turquoise Lake 142
61. West Dell Creek Falls 147

JACKSON

Introduction 149
62. Cache Creek/Game Creek 151
63. Goodwin Peak and Jackson Peak 152
64. Snow King 154

HOBACK CANYON & SOUTH JACKSON

Introduction 157
65. Cream Puff Peak 159
66. Monument Ridge 162
67. Ann's Ridge 163
68. Willow Creek 163
69. Cliff Creek Falls 165
70.. Munger Mountain 167
71. Wolf Mountain 168
72. Red Creek 171
73. Elk Mountain 173

Bibliography 174
Appendix 176
Index 188
Trekking in the Himalayas 195

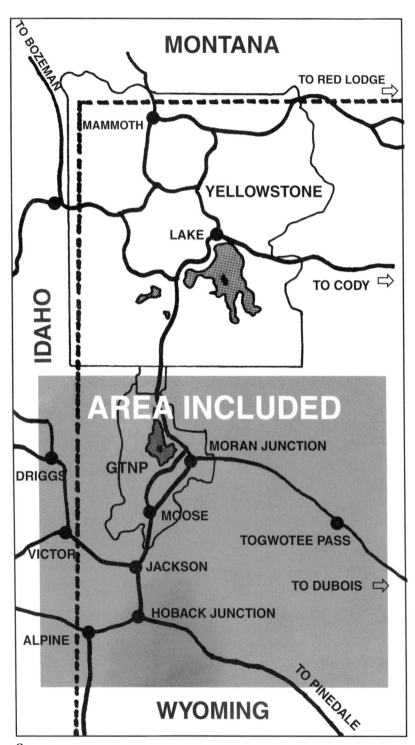

INTRODUCTION

▲

When a friend of mine from Ohio came to Jackson to visit a number of years ago, he was thunderstruck by the valley's innate beauty — or as he put it, "If the Almighty took vacations, this is where he'd go." Not very eloquent, but a common reaction. Jackson Hole has a long tradition of spellbinding those who enter its confines, from the earliest Indians and hunters to the tourists and residents of today's booming resort community.

One of the first visitors, fur trapper William Sublette, is credited with naming the valley in 1829. Turn-of-the-century trappers called valleys ringed by mountains "holes." It was accepted practice to name areas they frequented after themselves; hence, Pierre's Hole in Idaho, Ogden's Hole in Utah and Brown's Hole in Colorado. Sublette named the valley "Jackson's Hole" in honor of his partner, Davey Jackson. A tad indelicate for modern-day sensibilities, it is now called Jackson Hole.

Roughly 80 miles long and six to eight miles wide, the valley is ringed by Yellowstone National Park to the north, Togwotee Pass to the northeast, the Gros Ventre Range to the east, Hoback Canyon to the south, Teton Pass and the Snake River Range to the southwest, and, of course, the Teton Range to the west.

The Tetons sheer size, shape, and beauty are the most notable feature in the valley geologically and scenically. The Shoshone Indians called the range Teewinot, or many pinnacles; in 1811 William Price Hunt of the Astorians named them Pilot Knobs. Dr. Ferdinand Hayden said they resembled shark's teeth. Men on his 1872 expedition to the region named the highest peak Mt. Hayden in his honor. But it was the name three trappers from the Canadian North West Company applied that struck: Les Trois Tetons, or three breasts. The biggest breast became "the Grand Teton."

The range is one of the most precipitous in the world, completely lacking foothills. Along it's 40 mile course, it rises 3,000 - 7,000 feet from the sage-covered flats of the valley floor. The impressive upsweep of granite is an irresistible magnet to climbers and adventurers. The Grand Teton was first climbed in 1898, thirty-one years before the park was established. However there is some controversy over this, and it may have been climbed as early as 1872 by Nathaniel Langford and James Stevenson. Since that time an untold number of climbers and hikers have explored its peaks and 250 miles of trail.

Less impressive but just as beautiful in their own right are the national forest lands that ring the valley. The 287,000 acre wilderness area in the heart of the Gros Ventre is home to 20 peaks over 10,000 feet high, abundant wildlife, glacier-carved cliffs, and colorful polychrome rock bands. One hundred and ten miles of trails criss-cross this, some of the prettiest country in the region. Teton Wilderness and the Absaroka Range to the north straddle the Continental Divide. Source of both the Yellowstone and Snake rivers, that wilderness is almost 900 square miles in size. Targhee National Forest presides over the western side of the range. There, long U-shaped, glaciated canyons allow easier access up western slopes and afford dramatic views of the range as well.

Surrounded by one of the jewels of the National Park system and national forest land in every direction, Jackson Hole is in the enviable position of offering more backcountry to explore than virtually any other area in the lower 48 states.

HOW TO USE THIS BOOK

The hikes in this book have been arranged by geographical area. For each area, there is an introduction and a numbered map showing the approximate location of walks in that region. Hike descriptions begin with an information capsule at the top of the page, followed by a written narrative intended to give you a general feeling of the route.

The first component in the information capsule is distance. This is just what the name implies: the number of miles you will cover on the hike. For off-trail hikes the distance given is the best approximate available. The mileage is listed as either one-way or round-trip (RT). One-way mileage is given when the hiker is faced with several different options for a return, such as from the top of the aerial tram in Teton Village. If a hike has several obvious turn-around points enroute, round-trip mileage was broken out for the different turn-around points; the hike to Garnet Canyon and the Lower Saddle is an example.

The next category in the information capsule is elevation gained, followed by the maximum elevation. This information should help you determine how strenuous the hike will be, based upon the number of feet you ascend and how high you'll get. Both factors are important in assessing the time and energy needed for the trip. An average walking pace on level ground is two miles per hour. On steep terrain it drops to about 1.5 miles an hour. Altitude and uneven cross-country terrain further reduce speed.

The final information capsule item is maps. Unless otherwise noted all maps listed are USGS 7.5', 1:24,000 scale topographic quadrangles. The U.S. Forest Service publishes large maps of Targhee and Bridger-Teton National Forests. Maps of Grand Teton National Park are also available from the U.S. Geological Survey and several commercial companies. While their scale limits the amount of information available for specific hikes, these maps provide a good overview of the entire region. They can be purchased at local visitor centers and outdoor shops.

Following the information capsule a narrative describes each hike. The description includes directions to the trailhead, starting from the town of Jackson, and salient features you'll pass enroute. Again, internal mileages are best estimates.

REGULATIONS AND ETHICAL CONSIDERATIONS

We need solitude and space to roam, room to stretch both our legs and our souls. For years this has been met in the backcountry, where the beauty of alpine lakes, meadows and peaks — and the effort required to get there — elicits some of our best qualities. Now the solace and beauty of our wild areas is threatened by the sheer numbers of us seeking the same. Every year trails become more rutted, waterways more polluted, campsites more degraded by trash and half-burned logs and ash. Mother Nature no longer needs a Band-Aid: She's a candidate for triage.

If the backcountry is to survive it must be treated with greater care. It is your responsibility to know the Forest Service and National Park regulations concerning camping, fire, firearms, pets, livestock, hunting and fishing, etc. of the area you are entering. These are generally posted at trailheads or can be obtained at the appropriate visitor center. (Special note: A permit is needed for all backcountry camping in Grand Teton or Yellowstone National Park. These can be obtained at park headquarters as well as several other ranger stations).

While it is not my place to lecture, a few points merit special emphasis to help protect the resource.

Fires and campsite selection

Fires are prohibited in the backcountry of Grand Teton National Park and designated areas of the national forest. It is always preferable to use a lightweight backpacking stove, even if you are in an area that permits fires. In addition to eliminating the danger of forest fires, you won't impact the area with blackened rocks, half-burned wood, charcoal and ash. Carry and use a stove.

If you are camping in a heavily-trafficked area, select a site that is obviously used rather than impact a new area. If you are camping in a rarely visited area, select a site that has no evidence of prior use. Sites that have been lightly impacted — obviously used but with vegetation surviving on the site — should be avoided. If you don't re-use them they will probably recover.

In choosing a pristine site, stay away from trails and waterways. Avoid moist areas or vegetated forest floors and alpine zones that will register the impact of your feet. Look for rock outcroppings, gravel areas, or snow. Alternate the paths to water and your kitchen area to avoid formation of a use trail. Wear "soft" shoes around camp. Avoid using the same site more than one night. You'll know you've done a good job if,when you leave, no one can tell you've been there.

Sanitation and trash

It has long been believed that feces buried 6-8" deep is rapidly decomposed by surface soil organisms. Recent research has shown that it may be a year or more before decomposition occurs. This underscores the importance of defecating at least 200 feet away from trails, campsites, waterways and other frequently used places. What you leave is going to be there for a long time. Toilet paper should be burned if possible, with the remnants buried or packed out. Tampons should be packed out unless you are in grizzly country, in which case they may be burned in a hot fire.

To protect lakes and stream, minimize the use of biodegradable soap for bathing and dishes. Lather and rinse away from the water source with water carried to your site in a pot. This allows the soap to break down as it filters through the soil before re-entering the water system.

Aluminum does not burn, no matter how hot the fire. Don't attempt it unless you enjoy picking flakes of the stuff out of ashes. Pack it out. Pack out all your trash, including food scraps. Burying them doesn't cut it — animals dig them up. You're potentially affecting both their health and behavior patterns. Marmots were not meant to eat Top Ramen with Oriental sweet-and-sour sauce.

On the way out, when your pack is light and you're in great shape, pick up the gum wrappers, cans, foil and other items left by backcountry users who don't love the land as much as you do.

Backcountry Travel

Travel in the backcountry in a way that minimizes disturbance to wildlife and others. Unless you are in grizzly country, walk quietly. Avoid using bright colored clothes and equipment to cut down on the likelihood others will see you and your camp. (The exception to this, of course, is during hunting season.) When you take a break, move away from the trail to a durable area such as rock outcroppings so others can pass by without contact.

Respect the needs of wildlife. If you decide to approach an animal for a photograph or closer look, avoid sudden movement and stay downwind. If your behavior causes a reaction, you are too close. Keep in mind that you may cause an animal to abandon a nest or birthing site, water supply or feeding area — all of which have negative consequences. Allow animals plenty of space. It should go without saying that animals should never be "chased," yet I have witnessed this on more than one occasion by people intent upon getting a photograph. Many of the wildlife encounters in Yellowstone in recent years have been bison turning around and chasing their pursuers!

Finally, a word on trail travel. Walk in the middle of a path as much as possible, even if it's muddy. Walking on the edge of a trail to avoid a bog only makes the bog bigger by breaking down the trail edges and widening the mess. Similarly, snow patches on trails should be crossed rather than skirted to avoid creating small side trails. Trails switchback because the steepness of the slope and instability of the soils cannot hold a path that leads straight up. By shortcutting switchbacks, you're creating the very problem they were intended to avoid: erosion. Follow the trail.

Off-Trail Considerations

This book contains a number of unofficial routes and trails. Cross-country and off-trail travel demand a higher level of skill to protect both yourself and the environment. Check at the Jenny Lake Ranger Station before you go. The knowledgeable staff is up-to-date on current conditions and hazards of which you may not be aware.

Should you travel off-trail? If you do not know how to use a map and compass, safely cross steep talus and snow, render emergency first-aid, or effect a rescue from a remote area, the answer is probably no—your skill level is not sufficient to keep you safe. Either go with other people who possess these skills or stay on maintained trails until you have acquired them.

If you do travel off-trail, minimize your impact on the environment. Use an existing path if it exists. If not, spread out whenever possible, instead of walking single file, to avoid creating a new one. Even infrequent trampling can create an incipient trail, which will attract additional use. Choose a route that crosses durable surfaces such as rock or hard ground. Trails are more likely to develop on fragile vegetation, particularly above timberline. Avoid traveling in early season, when ground saturated from snowmelt deteriorates easily. Give the ground a chance to dry out. Don't mark your route by constructing cairns. Marking invites further use of that route, ultimately creating a new user trail. A prime example of this has occurred in Hanging Canyon. Finally, follow gradual ridges instead of cutting down steep slopes. If you must hike a steep slope, switchback to minimize erosion.

SAFETY IN THE HOLE

It is beyond the scope of this book, nor is it my intention, to detail safety aspects of backcountry travel: entire volumes have been written on the subject. Basic skills, hypothermia, dehydration, first aid, emergency response and rescue procedures are universal concerns best addressed elsewhere. There are, however, several considerations unique to Jackson Hole that merit mention.

The first of these is weather. Be aware that it can snow almost any day of the year in the region and over the course of time it probably has. Not only that, but it can snow on a day that begins with 80° on the thermometer and bright blue skies. Pictures from a July 4th trip to Green Lakes show me in a down jacket and wool hat, desperately clutching a mug of hot coffee to try to warm up as the snow swirls in the background. Cheers. Conversely, heat and sun can create dehydration and sunburn problems.

Be prepared to withstand sudden, severe weather changes in the mountains. On all but the simplest of hikes, and especially those at high altitude, you should carry a minimum of a wool hat and gloves, wind jacket, pile jacket or sweater, an emergency "space" blanket, sunscreen, sunglasses, a map and compass, and adequate food and water.

The second safety concern is altitude. The valley floor lies at

6,200 feet. In the Tetons, it is not uncommon to gain an additional 3,000-4,000 feet on a day hike. Hikers flying into the valley are literally going from sea level to 10,000 feet in a matter of hours. Our bodies are not capable of adjusting to less oxygen that quickly. Common symptoms of mild altitude illness include headaches, loss of appetite, a general "blah" feeling similar to the flu, poor sleep and nausea. Should these occur, drink plenty of water and don't gain any more elevation. If you are on a day hike the symptoms should disappear shortly after you descend to the valley floor. If you are on a multi-day trip and your symptoms do not abate overnight, the safest course is to descend.

The third safety concern is underestimating time and energy needed for a high altitude hike that gains significant elevation. In terms of effort, the 9.2 mile round-trip hike to Amphitheater and Surprise Lake, due to its almost 3,000 foot elevation gain, is equivalent to 15 miles of flat walking. As a rule of thumb, add an "effort mile" to the overall mileage for every 500 feet gained. This will give you a more realistic approximation of how much energy the hike really takes. Give yourself enough time for your intended destination. If the hike is taking longer than you anticipated, don't push yourself to exhaustion: turn around. Many accidents in the mountains are the result of people becoming overly tired and losing their physical and mental acuity.

Finally, giardia and other bacterial agents have become an increasing problem in the region's backcountry water supply. Unless you are sure the water is safe. it is recommended that you treat all surface water before drinking it.

A FINAL WORD

This book is intended to serve as a general reference to hiking trails in the valley, and not as a substitute for experience or one's own route finding abilities and skills. While reference points and intersections have been carefully selected to aid hikers, field conditions often change. This book should be used only as a reference and not as the final word in situations that require judgment calls. This guide is also not intended to be a comprehensive survey of what is available, but an introduction to the different areas of the valley. It is my hope that it will lead hikers to explore the entire valley, not just the more popular eastern side of the Tetons. Yes, by all means, hike the spectacular canyons and meadows of those jagged peaks. Do these trips — then go find the rest of the valley.

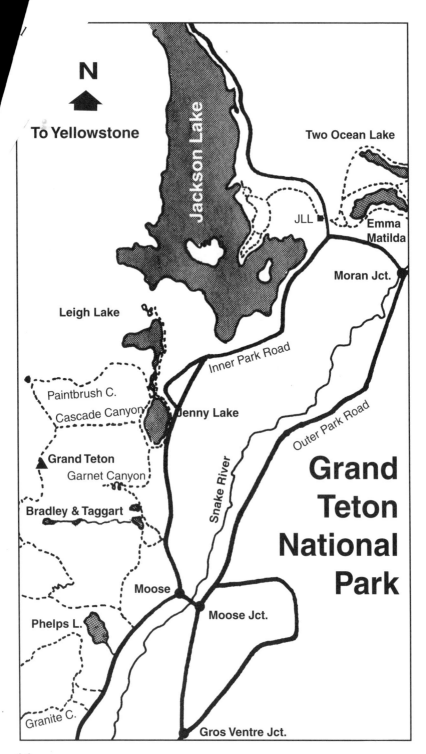

Grand Teton National Park
▲

It has been said that the Tetons look like mountains should—rugged, snow-capped peaks rising thousands of feet above the valley floor without foothills to lessen the impact. At 13,770 feet, the Grand Teton crowns the breathtaking range, drawing over a million hikers, climbers and sightseers to admire it every year.

This, the youngest range in the Rocky Mountains, extends in a north-south direction for 40 miles and forms the heart of Grand Teton National Park and western boundary of Jackson Hole. The peaks rise 3,000 to 7,000 feet above the valley, soaring above treeline to craggy pinnacles and snowfields. They contain over a dozen glaciers, remnants of the last ice age 9,000 years ago. Ten summits tower over 12,000 feet. An additional 18 top the 11,000 foot mark. Many of these giants are tightly grouped between Avalanche and Cascade canyons, creating one of the most spectacular alpine vistas in the world.

At the base of the high peaks and deep, glacial-carved canyons that cut through the range lie seven piedmont lakes. From Phelps Lake northward they include Taggart, Bradley, Jenny, String, Leigh and Jackson lakes. These deep blue sapphires are ringed with lodgepole pine on their eastern shores and thick, shady forests of Engelmann spruce and Douglas fir to the west. The 24.5 mile Valley Trail skirts most of them, starting at Teton Village and crossing several glacial moraines while traveling north to Bearpaw Lake.

The valley floor is covered with sage and meadowlands. Moose, black bear, elk, antelope, coyotes and deer are frequently seen in the park's lowlands. Among the smaller animals, pikas, rabbits, marmots and ground squirrels are common. Trumpeter swans and bald eagles head the popularity list of more than 200 species of birds in Grand Teton.

The park was established on February 26, 1929, by an act of Congress. It was only a third of its present size, covering roughly 150 square miles, and excluded parts of the range and most of the valley floor. It was expanded to its present size in 1950, with over a fifth of the additional 348 square miles donated by John D. Rockefeller, Jr. Appalled by the dancehalls, saloons and other developments near Jenny Lake, Rockefeller had quietly been acquiring land adjoining the park to protect it from development and then donated it to the park expansion effort.

There are over 250 miles of hiking trails in the park. With the exception of those on the valley floor, most routes tend to gain elevation rapidly, switchbacking up steep slopes and canyons. The trail up Death Canyon is one of the steepest; the trail to the Forks of Cascade Canyon is one of the easier grades. Low-lying trails are usually free of snow by mid-July. High trails can have patches of snow as late as early August. The highest point of maintained trail in the park is 10,800 foot Static Peak Divide, closely followed by Paintbrush Divide at 10,720 feet.

All overnight backcountry camping requires a permit. Persons interested in off-trail hiking and scrambling must register with the Jenny Lake Ranger Station in the park. Their summer telephone number is 307-739-3343. For information on current hiking conditions, rules and regulations, and securing a free backpacking permit contact:

                Permit Office
                Grand Teton National Park
                Moose, Wyoming 83012
                307-733-3309

1 PHELPS LAKE
2 DEATH CANYON/STATIC PEAK

Distance:
    Phelps Lake Overlook: .9 miles one-way
    Patrol Cabin: 3.7 miles one-way
    Static Peak Divide: 6.7 miles one-way
    Static Peak: 7 miles one-way
Elevation gain:
    Phelps Lake Overlook: 420 ft.
    Patrol Cabin: 1061 ft.
    Static Peak Divide: 4020 ft.
    Static Peak: 4523 ft.
Maximum elevation:
    Phelps Lake Overlook: 7,200 ft.
    Patrol Cabin: 7,841 ft.
    Static Peak Divide: 10,800 ft.
    Static Peak: 11,303 ft.
Maps:
    Grand Teton
    Mount Bannon

People who have backpacked up Death Canyon to Static Peak Divide think the canyon is well-named: Death is exactly what they feel like when they reach the Divide 4,000 plus feet above the valley floor. The view helps resurrect them. From the top of Static Peak (only .3 miles further and 500 feet higher) impressive Buck Mountain looks close enough to touch. The Grand Teton looms to the north and the valley floor stretches out to the east. Prospector's Mountain lies to the south; the aquamarine teardrop named Timberline Lake rests directly below. And, of course, there's the view into the U-shaped glacial defile that is Death Canyon itself. Reportedly it was named after a member of an early surveying party who wandered into the canyon and never returned. Shorter forays into the canyon include pleasant trips to both Phelps Lake Overlook and the Death Canyon Patrol Cabin.

Drive 12 miles north of Jackson on U.S. 89/191 to Moose Junction. Turn left and go roughly one mile to the junction with the Moose-Wilson Road on your left. Turn here and continue three more miles to the White Grass Ranch intersection on your right. This narrow paved road soon deteriorates into a potholed dirt artery that leads to a trailhead parking area 1.5 miles from the intersection. The signed trailhead is at the parking lot's west end.

Phelps Lake Overlook

Old-growth pine stretches high above you at the start of the relatively easy trail leading into Death Canyon. Numerous small streams contribute to the lushness of first the forest floor, then the open meadows as you gradually begin to climb the morainal ridge to the overlook.

Lacey cow parsnip, royal purple monkshood, magenta monkeyflowers, delicate mauve sticky geraniums, and Indian paintbrush ranging in color from deep rose to fiery red-orange compete for your attention during the peak bloom of mid-summer. Come fall, tiny lavender astors, goldenrod, and deep pink fireweed steal the show.

Near the end of the clearing the trail tops the moraine at 7,200 foot Phelps Lake Overlook, almost 600 feet above the pocket of water left by Death Canyon Glacier 9,000 years ago. At the far east end of the lake, almost hidden in the trees, is the famous JY Ranch. Built in 1908 by Louis H. Joy, the JY was one of the valley's first dude ranches. It is now privately owned by the Rockefeller family. The lake, home to native cutthroat, is named after a trapper who reported the its existence to members of the 1872 Hayden Expedition. In summer, moose frequent the west end of Phelps Lake and its marshes.

Death Canyon Patrol Cabin

From Phelps Lake Overlook, the trail descends almost 600 feet in three switchbacks above the lake's western shore. At 1.6 miles, you pass a junction to Open Canyon and the Valley Trail to the left (E). Turn right (W) here and begin a gradual ascent through Engelmann spruce and cottonwood trees to the entrance of Death Canyon. The trail steepens after about one-mile and switchbacks up the canyon's north side. Near the end of the switchbacks it passes close beneath the glaciated canyon's steep rock walls, where ancient schists and gneisses are exposed.

At the top of the switchbacks the canyon opens up into meadow and forests of whitebark pine. The trail then follows the main stream in the canyon to the Death Canyon Patrol Cabin, which is 3.7 miles from the trailhead. A pleasant, meadowed area, the cabin makes a good turn-around point for a shorter day hike.

Static Peak Divide and Static Peak

Beyond the Death Canyon Patrol Cabin the trail forks left (W) towards Fox Creek Pass, reached 9.2 miles from the White Grass trailhead. Take the right fork (N) to access Static Peak Divide and Static Peak. This steep trail gains almost 3,000 feet in three miles to reach the Divide, the highest point of maintained trail in the park. It is often snow-covered until late in the season: check with the Jenny Lake Ranger Station to assess conditions before departing.

Less than a quarter-mile from the patrol cabin the trail begins its steep ascent up open slopes, staying to the right of a rushing stream before crossing it roughly one mile from the trail junction and winding up steep switchbacks. At 5.9 miles, just past treeline, you reach a small saddle with great views of the valley floor. Here the trail swings north and ascends a long, rocky ridge another .8 miles to

The view as you descend Phelps Overlook towards the junction with Death Canyon Trail.

Static Peak Divide.

To climb Static Peak, leave the trail and walk right several yards. You'll soon see an unofficial trail winding through the talus of Static Peak's southern slopes. It gains roughly 500 feet in the .3 miles to the summit of the 11,303 foot peak, named for to its propensity to attract electricity. While the rubble covered southern slopes are a non-technical walk, Static Peak's northern side drops steeply into the chasm separating it from Buck Mountain.

The latter, an impressive 11,938 foot peak, is the showpiece of the southern end of the Teton Range. It was first climbed in 1898 by mapmaker Thomas Bannon and his assistant George Buck, for whom the peak was named. For many years the peak was called Mt. Alpenglow because its southern side catches and holds the last light of the day.

3 TAGGART & BRADLEY LAKES

Distance:
  3.75 miles RT
Elevation gain:
  500 ft.
Maximum elevation:
  7,125 ft.
Maps:
  Moose
  Grand Teton

Bradley and Taggart Lakes lie at the base of the Tetons between Avalanche and Garnet canyons. The two pretty, glacial lakes are evidence of the last ice age over 9,000 years ago. Glaciers grinding down the canyons began dropping dirt and rock as their forward progress slowed at the base of the range. The deposited debris formed ridges of earth called moraines. These held the meltwater in place, creating today's lakes.

In 1985, a lightning-caused fire burned much of the lodgepole forest surrounding the trail to the two lakes. The burn opened up views of the Tetons and clearly exposed the moraines. Although charred trees scar the hillsides, it is interesting to view the effects of the fire and subsequent regeneration of the area. Nutrients returned to the soil by the blaze have created lush, flower-filled meadows, while the downed trees have attracted increased numbers of insects and the birds which prey on them. Both woodpeckers and owls abound in the burned forest.

Drive 12 miles north of Jackson on U.S. Hwy. 89/191 to Moose Junction. Turn left and drive past park headquarters to the Moose Entrance of Grand Teton National Park. From the entrance it is three miles to the well-signed Taggart and Bradley Lake parking area on the left-hand side of the road.

Walk west across the sage-covered flats to a fork in the trail. The left fork leads to Beaver Creek, start of a four mile loop hike past the outlet of Taggart Lake — a possible alternative to the hike described below.

The right fork skirts the base of the moraine, crosses a bridge over Taggart Creek, then begins a gradual ascent up a gully that stays to the right of the fast mountain stream fed by both Taggart Lake and Avalanche Canyon to the west. The Grand Teton, formerly obscured by trees, towers above the charred trunks still standing on the forest floor.

At 1.1 miles, the route to the lakes divides and you may head in either direction to complete the loop. For purpose of description, stay left and walk through the burned forest to Taggart Lake at 1.6 miles. The clear, blue-green water of the lake often re-

The Grand Teton reflected in Taggart Lake. For a map of the hike, see page 24.

flects the mountains and offers good fishing. As the lakes are part of the park's water supply, swimming is prohibited.

The loop trail connecting the lakes heads right (N) to Bradley, following Taggart's eastern shore until it climbs the lateral moraine separating the two bodies of water. After switchbacking to the top, it drops about 100 feet down to Bradley Lake. From there the trail back to the parking area re-ascends the moraine and turns left (S).

It is also possible to continue on the trail above the east side of Bradley, cross another lateral moraine at 1.5 miles and intersect the trail leading to Surprise and Amphitheater Lakes.

The two lakes were named after members of Hayden's 1872 expedition to this area. Frank Bradley, chief geologist for the expedition, drown while trying to find a ford across the Snake River. W.R. Taggart was an assistant geologist for the same expedition. He first visited Jackson Hole in 1860 as a member of a survey for the U.S. Army Engineers led by Capt. W.F. Raynolds.

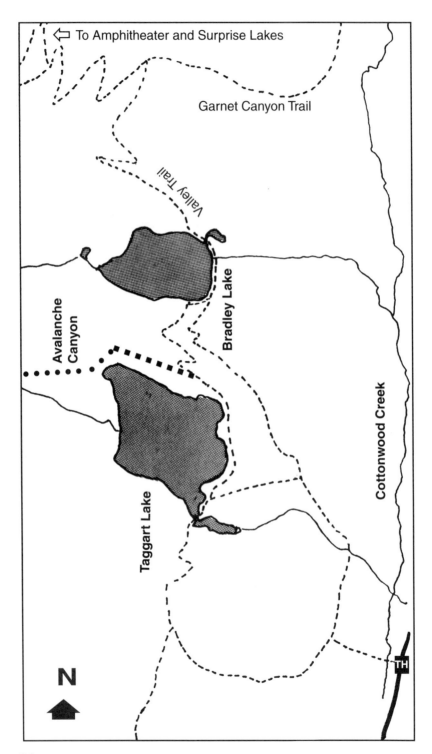

4 AVALANCHE CANYON

Distance:
  Lake Taminah: 10 miles RT
  Snowdrift Lake: 12 miles RT
Elevation gain:
  Lake Taminah: 2,455 ft.
  Snowdrift Lake: 3,383 ft.
Maximum elevation:
  Lake Taminah: 9,080 ft.
  Snowdrift Lake: 10,006 ft.
Maps:
  Moose
  Grand Teton

Accessed only by rough game trails, Avalanche Canyon is the least visited major canyon in the park. Climbers walk up it to approach routes on Buck Mountain, Mount Wister, Nez Perce, Cloudveil Dome and the South Teton. Hikers are drawn to its isolation, Shoshoko Falls and high alpine lakes surrounded by snow-covered peaks. Pioneer Teton guide Paul Petzoldt called the hike "one of the most beautiful in the entire United States."

The cross-country route begins at a popular trailhead. Drive 12 miles north of Jackson on U.S. 89/191 to the Moose Junction. Turn left and drive west for another four miles, past park headquarters and the Moose entrance station, to the Taggart and Bradley lakes parking area, which is on the left-hand side of the road.

Begin walking on the well-signed trail to Taggart Lake, traversing a broad meadow before swinging right and crossing a bridge spanning Taggart Creek. At 1.6 miles, you'll reach Taggart Lake. See that hike for further detail.

Avalanche Canyon and Shoshoko Falls are clearly visible from Taggart's eastern shore. The trail continues north, heading towards Bradley Lake. Just before the trail begins to switchback up the glacial moraine separating the two lakes, you'll see a large, dead fallen tree to your left. An unofficial use trail begins below the tree. This small but distinctive human/animal path heads west towards the canyon. Following the north side of Taggart Creek, it winds first through several boggy areas, then willow and brush as it gains elevation.

The intermittent trail stays to the right side of Taggart Creek, which forks near several large boulders roughly 4.5 miles and 1,100 feet above the parking area. The left fork of the creek heads to the base of Buck Mountain. Following the right (N) side of the creek through the brush, willows and talus will bring you to Shoshoko Falls, a frothy cascade that flows from the outlet of 9,080 foot Lake Taminah perched above you. To reach the lake, walk to the right of the falls and ascend either the rock slabs or gullies until you are level with its top. Often there will be a large snowfield here. Traverse left (S), using care if snow is present, to reach the rim of the lake, five miles from your starting point.

If you wish to continue to Snowdrift Lake, an additional mile and almost 1,000 feet above Lake Taminah, hike along the north shore to the rocky meadow at Lake Taminah's west end and then follow the right side of the obvious drainage. Near the top of the drainage veer left (S) to gain access to the bench that circles the lake. Good camping spots can be found on its north side.

Following an average winter there is usually a significant amount of snow from the high, timberless country around the lakes all the way to the upper reaches of Avalanche Canyon. If you do not know how to safely negotiate steep snow it is best to stop at Shoshoko Falls.

Hikers attempting to reach the lakes should also be aware that, true to its name, the canyon is frequently swept by snow in the spring and early summer. During the winter of 1985-86 huge slides uprooted dozens of trees, making cross-country travel a slow proposition.

▲

5 COTTONWOOD CREEK

Distance:
    1.6 miles
Elevation gain:
    Negligible
Maximum elevation:
    Approx. 6,700 ft.
Maps:
    Moose

The short, cross-country walk along Cottonwood Creek to Geraldine Lucas Rock is a good half-day choice for fishermen, young children, history buffs, and those who lack mountain lungs. It's also a serene place to observe bulging elk cutting across the quiet meadows on frosty fall evenings.

To reach the starting point, drive 12 miles north of Jackson on U.S. Hwy. 89/191 to Moose Junction. Turn left and drive past park headquarters to the Moose Entrance of Grand Teton National Park. From the entrance it is 3.2 miles to the Cottonwood Creek Picnic Area on your right. Park here and walk across the road.

Follow the wood buckrail fence until it turns left (W). Continue walking straight (N) here. Cut through the meadow, framed by the Grand Teton and neighboring peaks to your left, Cottonwood Creek to your right. The

Visiting the old Lucas Ranch and Geraldine Lucas Rock is one of the highlights of the hike along Cottonwood Creek.

beauty of the walk is heightened in early to mid-summer, when sweet-smelling lupine reaches peak bloom and paints the fields shades of indigo, periwinkle and lavender.

At .4 miles, you intersect the dirt road leading to the Climber's Ranch. Walk south on the road until you see a bridge spanning the creek. Just above it on the left side of the road is a wide grassy spot used for parking by anglers. A use trail along the same heads north from the parking area. (If you are time-crunched, you can shorten this walk .4 miles one-way by driving 3.6 miles north from the park entrance to the Climber's Ranch. Turn unto the road, cross the bridge, and park in the aforementioned spot.)

The trail follows clear Cottonwood Creek, aptly named for the lovely trees that grace its banks. There are many good picnic spots enroute, but you may wish to eat at the old Lucas Ranch. Continue walking north until the trail peters out in open meadow. Ahead are the surviving buildings of the old ranch, now government property. Posted signs clearly remind visitors not to enter the buildings or remove artifacts, but the structures are fun to walk around, and give one a hint of what a former guest ranch was like.

In the early 1900s, the ranch was owned by Geraldine Lucas, a feisty, outspoken woman who frequently lodged climbers in the 1920s. At the age of 59, she decided to have a crack at the high peaks herself. On August 19, 1924, she and three men successfully climbed the Grand. She unfurled an American flag at the 13,770 foot summit and posed for the camera.

Geraldine was the first Jackson Hole woman to ascend the peak, the second overall. Eleanor Davis claimed first ascent honors for women less than a year earlier, when she and Albert Ellingwood successfully summitted the Owen-Spalding Route on August 27, 1923.

Lucas was one of many valley residents adamantly opposed to park expansion. She is on record saying Rockefeller—whose Snake River Land Company purchased land later donated to the park—would not get her off her land. When she died in 1938, her son Russell sold the property to a neighbor, who eventually did sell to Rockefeller.

But perhaps Geraldine Lucas was right: She remained on her land. A number of years after her death, her ashes were buried under a large rock on her former property. The site is marked by a plaque. To see it, walk west towards the mountains from the ranch buildings. Cut through a stretch of woods and head towards a solitary boulder in the meadow. The plaque is cemented into the top of the boulder.

▲

The Grand Teton dominates the view to the north from the Lower Saddle.

6 GARNET CANYON
7 LOWER SADDLE

Distance:
   The Meadows and Spalding Falls: 10 miles RT
   Lower Saddle: 14 miles RT
Elevation gain:
   To the Meadows: 1,312 ft.
   To Top of Spalding Falls: 2,312 ft.
   To the Lower Saddle: 4,912 ft.
Maximum elevation:
   The Meadows: approx. 9,000 ft.
   Top of Spalding Falls: 10,000 ft.
   Lower Saddle: 11,600 ft.
Maps:
   Moose
   Grand Teton

A walk up Garnet Canyon to the Meadows takes you from the valley floor to a magnificent alpine basin that serves as the jumping-off point for climbs up the South, Middle, Grand and other Teton peaks. There is no better view of the Middle Teton, with its distinctive black diabase dike, anywhere in the range.

For trailhead directions and a description of the first three miles of this hike, please refer to the description for Amphitheater and Surprise Lakes, hike no. 8.

When you reach the Garnet Trail junction, take the left fork. The trail climbs for a short distance beyond the junction, then levels out and actually drops as it traverses south facing slopes and enters the canyon, overlooking a steep drop-off and Garnet Creek far below. Early in the season the creek is an icy torrent fed by run-off from Nez Perce, Cloudveil Dome and the surrounding peaks.

The trail soon begins climbing again, turning into a rocky path as it switchbacks up the talus slopes. It officially ends at 8,800 feet at Garnet Creek Cascade (called Cleft Falls on the map), 1.1 miles beyond the Garnet Trail junction. Returning to Lupine Meadows from here makes for an 8.2 mile venture.

From the end of the trail a route marked by cairns heads west through a short boulder field to a rough path along Garnet Creek. The Meadows, a grassy alpine basin carpeted with flowers, is reached .6 miles from the end of the trail. Here the Middle Teton looms in front of you. To the right Spalding Falls gracefully arcs over 80 feet down to the Meadows floor. It was named in honor of Bishop Frank Spalding, who accompanied William Owen on the first ascent of the Grand Teton in 1898.

The Meadows and falls are a good ending destination for most hikers.

To the Saddle:

Strong, experienced parties with good scrambling/route finding skills occasionally continue to the Lower Saddle. This is a long, arduous route that involves climbing a fixed rope below the Saddle's headwall. It should not be attempted by those who lack sufficient experience.

The route to the Saddle heads up the steep hillside towards the falls. The loose dirt and stone trail passes near its right side before switchbacking above it to a small level area dubbed Petzoldt's Caves. The "caves" are dirt camping spots under the overhang of several large boulders. In the 1930s and 40s mountain guide Paul Petzoldt dug out space under the boulders to shelter overnight clients preparing to climb the Grand the following day.

Above the caves, route is marked by cairns and heads generally northwest to the morainal ridges leading to the headwall. When in doubt, stay to the right. You'll cross a stream tumbling down from the base of Teepee Pillar just before entering the main moraine. Jackson Hole Mountain Guides' base camp is located above you. The route to the Saddle heads almost due west: if you head north you're likely on a trail to JHMG's tent camp.

The upper moraine ends at the steep, rocky headwall. The National Park Service maintains a heavy hemp "fixed rope" at the headwall to help climbers ascend the band of cliffs. In early season the bottom of the rope is often frozen in snow and ice, forcing a climb up the adjacent snowfields. Bring an ice axe and know how to use it! As the snow begins to melt you may find yourself in a steady shower of icy water as you climb hand over hand up the slippery rope and rock. Proceed very carefully: a fall here could be disasterous.

Above the rope the trail first traverses south towards a potable spring, then west up to the 11,600 foot Lower Saddle between the Middle and Grand Tetons. The National Park Service and Exum Mountain Guides maintain huts on the Saddle. Although both are used for rescue operations, neither are open to the general public.

The Saddle is home to fragile alpine vegetation (please stay on the trails), pikas, and an army of marmots. East, the vista encompasses the valley floor, Gros Ventre, Wind River, and Wyoming ranges. Pierre's Hole, the green and brown patchwork of Idaho farmland, and distant Lehmi mountains lie west. The Grand dominates the north.

Return via the same route. It is possible to descend the west side of the Saddle into Dartmouth Basin and return to the valley floor via Cascade Canyon. The descent is on dangerously loose, steep rock. For this reason it is generally avoided. If you are considering this option, please check at the Jenny Lake Ranger Station for current conditions.

Spalding Falls marks the western end of The Meadows.

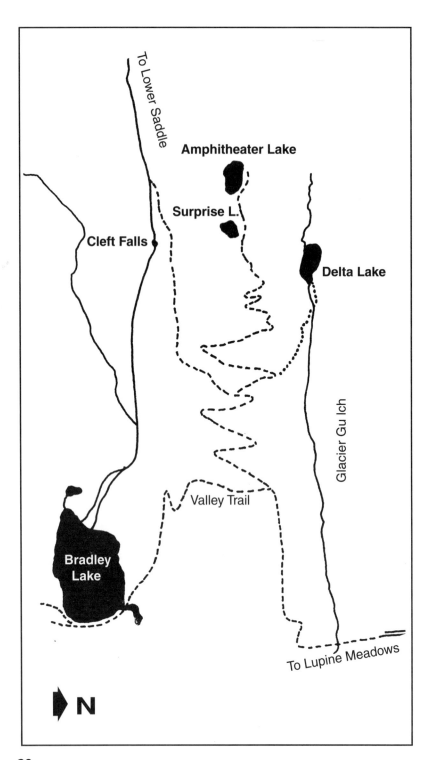

8 AMPHITHEATER & SURPRISE LAKES

Distance:
  Surprise: 9.2 miles RT
  Amphitheater: 9.6 miles RT
Elevation gained:
  Surprise: 2,810 ft.
  Amphitheater: 2,960 ft.
Maximum elevation:
  9,698 ft.
Maps:
  Moose
  Grand Teton

A high cirque, alpine lakes and nice views of Jackson Hole on the way up make the Glacier Trail to Surprise and Amphitheater Lakes one of the most popular in Grand Teton National Park. Since the first three miles of the 4.8 mile trail is also the approach for many standard climbing routes up the Grand Teton, expect to see lots of people enroute. Starting early will alleviate the feeling that you're traveling on a freeway of daypacks, but be forewarned that this is not a good choice if your goal is solitude in the mountains. The trail is also not recommended if this is your first day in the area, as it rises nearly 3,000 feet in a short distance. Give yourself several days to adjust to the altitude before attempting to climb the 14 switchbacks leading to the lakes!

To reach the trailhead, drive 12 miles north of Jackson on U.S. Hwy 89/191 to Moose Junction. Turn left and drive past park headquarters to the Moose Entrance Station of Grand Teton National Park. The Lupine Meadows Junction is roughly six miles north of the entrance station. Turn left at that junction and follow the road across a bridge. Go left just past the bridge, then stay right (W) where a side road shortly turns off to park employee cabins. Follow the signs to the parking area; the trail begins at the south end of the lot.

You'll walk a mile through marshy lowland before beginning a gradual climb up a wooded morainal ridge. At 1.7 miles (7,260 feet), the Glacier Trail intersects the Valley Trail, which leads to Bradley Lake. Above the signed intersection angle left. The trail soon begins to zig-zag up the face between Glacier Gulch and Garnet Canyon in a series of long switchbacks. These open slopes can be a cooker on hot days, with little shade to provide relief from the beating sun. Be sure to bring plenty of water. Fucshia monkeyflowers, purple monkshood, red Indian paintbrush and white cow parsnip — wildflowers that thrive in moist environments — are found at small rivulets crossing the trail at .3 miles. Further up the hillside the ubiquitous yellow blooms of balsamroot and heartleaf arnica provide splashes of color.

Taggart and Bradley Lakes on the valley floor and Jackson Peak to the east come into view as you ascend the 1.3 miles of trail between the first intersection and Garnet Trail Junction, three miles from the starting point. From here the left fork leads to Garnet Canyon. The right fork leads to Surprise and Amphitheater lakes via a series of 14 shorter, mostly wooded switchbacks. Surprise Lake is nestled at 9,550 feet, and like Amphitheater 148 feet above, it is frozen much of the year. Scramble up the easy pinnacle southeast of the lake's outlet for good views.

Amphitheater is only .2 miles above Surprise Lake. It is reached by the trail around the north side of Surprise. This lake lies in a cirque at the base of 11,618 foot Disappointment Peak. The peak received its moniker after a 1925 party of climbers thought they could reach the Grand by climbing up from the lake, only to find a huge gap between the summit of "Disappointment" and the Grand.

The trail to the lakes was constructed by Gibb Scott and Homer Richards in 1923 as a means to get guided horseback trips and climbers up to Teton Glacier. It was widely used throughout the 1920s since it was one of the few trails in the area. Traffic leveled out in the mid-1930s when the CCC completed the Garnet Canyon Trail, offering a viable alternative to the Grand Teton and opening access to many other peaks.

The view east of Amphitheater and Surprise lakes from the slopes of Disappointment Peak above them.

9 DELTA LAKE

Distance:
    3.8 miles one-way
Elevation gain:
    2,370 ft.
Maximum elevation:
    9,110 ft.
Maps:
    Moose
    Grand Teton

Snug against the base of the east side of the Grand Teton and Mount Owen, Delta Lake is a small alpine jewel framed by the two highest peaks in the Teton Range. The turquoise-colored body of water gets its striking color and name from the silt funneled into its west end by Teton Glacier above it.

Although one of the prettiest lake destinations in the high country, the lake is serendipitously lightly visited. Its quietude is fostered by a steady climb to the site, reached only after leaving an official trail and picking a route up its rocky outflow. Those without some route-finding ability and map reading skill should not attempt it.

The hike to Delta begins at the trailhead to Amphitheater and Surprise Lakes. Drive 12 miles north of Jackson on U.S. Hwy. 89/191 to Moose Junction. Turn left and drive past park headquarters on your right to the Moose Entrance station of Grand Teton National Park. From the entrance, it is roughly six miles to the Lupine Meadows turn-off on the left side of the road.

Turn at Lupine Meadows and cross a bridge over Cottonwood Creek. Go left just past the bridge; stay right where a side road shortly splits off to park employee housing. Follow the signs to the parking area. The trail begins at the south, or far, end of the lot.

The first three miles of trail to Garnet Junction are described in the hike write-up for Amphitheater and Surprise Lakes on page 33. At Garnet Junction, walk right (N) towards the lakes. At the end of the first switchback, drop steeply off the trail down a short wooded section, then contour northwest through the trees. Stay high until you see large boulders straddling the lake's rocky outflow. Angle towards them, staying high. When you reach the boulders scramble up them to the lake, unseen until you are at its lip.

By walking left along the south shore of the lake, it is possible to scramble up a steep hillside and drop south to Amphitheater and Surprise Lakes. It is also feasible to continue west then north above the lake for a "summit" view of the area.

10 JENNY LAKE
11 STRING LAKE
12 LEIGH AND BEARPAW LAKES

Distance:
  Jenny Lake: 6.6 miles RT
  String Lake: 3.6 miles RT
  Leigh Lake: 8.6 miles RT
  Bearpaw Lake: 7.8 miles RT
Elevation gained:
  Jenny Lake: Negligible
  String Lake: 309 ft.
  Leigh and Bearpaw lakes: 311 ft.
Maximum elevation:
  Jenny Lake: 6,820 ft.
  String Lake: 6,875 ft.
  Leigh and Bearpaw lakes: 6,877 ft.
Maps:
  Mount Moran
  Jenny Lake

Some of the most popular trails in Grand Teton National Park originate from the Jenny Lake/String Lake/Leigh Lake area. Their sparkling blue waters reflect the rocky spires of Teewinot, the Grand Teton, Mt. Owen and Mt. Moran. Shallow String Lake is believed to be an old river channel. It connects Jenny Lake to the south with Leigh Lake to the north. The latter is named after "Beaver Dick" Leigh, a colorful mountain man who made his living trapping in canyons on the west side of the Tetons. He forayed into the east side of the range often enough to be hired as a guide for the 1872 Hayden Expedition to Yellowstone and Jackson Hole.

Jenny Lake is named in honor of Leigh's Shoshone wife. She and the couple's six children died of smallpox during Christmas week of 1876. Several years later, already past 50, Leigh married a 14-year-old Bannock girl and fathered three more children before dying in 1899.

This trio of lakes can be reached from the String Lake outlet parking area. Drive 12 miles north of Jackson on U.S. Hwy 89/191 to Moose Junction. Turn left and drive past park headquarters to the Moose Entrance to Grand Teton National Park. Ten miles from the entrance station, turn left at String Lake Junction and drive 1.5 miles to the String Lake parking area on the right. The parking area itself is .4 miles long. Mileage for the hike around Jenny Lake is calculated from the String Lake outlet bridge at the south end of the lot. Mileage for the String and Leigh Lake hikes is figured from the north end of the lot.

Jenny Lake

Jenny Lake (6,783 feet) was formed by a glacier that flowed out of Cascade Canyon at the end of the last ice age 9,000 years ago. As the glacier began to melt at the base of the canyon it dropped rock debris it had carried down from Cascade's upper reaches, forming a terminal moraine that subsequently held in the glacier's meltwater. Jackson, Leigh, Bradley, Taggart and Phelps lakes were all formed in the same manner. Second only to Jackson Lake in size, Jenny is one mile wide and 1.5 miles long. It's deepest point measures 236 feet.

From the parking area, cross the bridge at String Lake outlet and follow the trail .3 miles to the junction with String Lake Trail. Stay left, walking southwest above the lake through forests of alpine fur and large Engelmann spruce. At 1.5 miles the slightly rolling, wooded trail drops to the lakeshore and crosses a stream rushing down from Hanging Canyon. The Cathedral Group looms ahead of you, named because this vantage point makes three of the major Teton Peaks look like one mountain, a "cathedral" with dozens of spires. Craggy Mt. Teewinot is in the forefront, the Grand Teton is in the middle background, and Mt. Owen is on the right.

At 1.7 miles, the trail passes the west shore boat dock. From here, it is only a half mile up a marked side trail to Hidden Falls. Many hikers take the east shore boat shuttle across the lake, making the falls a one mile roundtrip venture. Continue walking along the southwest shore. One mile past the junction to the falls, you'll pass Moose Ponds Overlook. In late afternoon it is common to see moose and occasionally beaver from this spot.

The trail leaves the woods as it turns at the overlook and drops towards the east shore boat dock and the footbridge crossing the south Jenny Lake outlet at 3.7 miles. From here, it is a 2.9 mile walk in-and-out of lodgepole forest back to the String Lake parking area. The trail closely follows the lakeshore, offering spectacular views up Cascade Canyon, the deepest in the park.

String Lake

Barely 10 feet deep and just over a football field in width, String Lake is one of the few lakes at the base of the Tetons warmed enough by the sun to make swimming more than a jump in-jump out proposition. The level trail around it can be easily walked in a couple of hours and offers good views of Mount Moran to the north and the Cathedrals to the south.

From the north end of the parking area, the trail winds through the trees on the east end of the lake. At .9 miles it crosses the bridge over Leigh Lake outlet and forks at a signed junction. The unmaintained trail to the right follows the west shore of Leigh Lake to the mouth of Leigh Canyon. That is often wet and Leigh Canyon itself is not trailed. Follow the left fork as it gently climbs above String Lake, hugging the slope of Rockchuck Peak. The trail intersects the trail to Paintbrush Canyon at 1.7 miles. Continue straight ahead at the junction, descending slightly through meadows and woods. In about a mile you'll pass an unmarked trail on the right that cuts steeply up open slopes. This leads to Laurel Lake, nestled at the bottom of the drainage between Rockchuck Peak to the north and Mount St. John on the south. The pretty little lake is a nice half-mile side trip that offers a quiet place to eat lunch.

Three miles around the lake you'll intersect the Jenny Lake trail going to the right. Turn left and follow the trail back to the south end of the parking area. A trail follows the lake back to the north end of the parking lot.

Leigh and Bearpaw lakes

The shores of Leigh Lake offer some of the best views of Mount Moran in the park. That massive peak towers over 3,000 feet above the lakeshore, its rocky slopes calmly reflected in the still waters. Falling Ice Glacier, a field of ice over 100 feet thick that hangs between Moran's East and West Horns, discharges glacial flour into the lake, giving Leigh its distinctive green hue. Two miles long and almost 250 feet deep, it is fed by streams tumbling down Leigh and Paintbrush canyons.

Follow the directions for the String Lake hike to the outlet at the north end of String Lake at .9 miles. Instead of crossing the bridge, the trail cuts back to the right and continues along Leigh's east lakeshore. There are several abandoned trails in the area. Stay on the one closest to the lake to avoid confusion. At 3.1 miles you'll come to a long series of sand and gravel beaches. There are numerous backcountry campsites located here. (These beaches are appealing, but since the sites are relatively close to a heavily-trafficked trail, a nicer alternative for campers is to use the trail and sites on the west side of the lake.) Mystic Isle is the large island at this end. Keep a sharp eye out for osprey which nest in the dead snags on its south side.

The trail follows the lake to its north end and a trail junction at 3.7 miles. The trail to Bearpaw Lake heads north (R), reaching the lake in .2 mile. To reach Trapper Lake, stay left. That lake is reached in another .6 miles. Both offer good fishing and few people.

North of Trapper an abandoned trail connects with Moran Bay on Jackson Lake. It is hard to follow, particularly near Moran Creek, but does offer good access to a nice backcountry site on Bearpaw Bay that otherwise require approach by boat.

The view from Jenny Lake Outlet

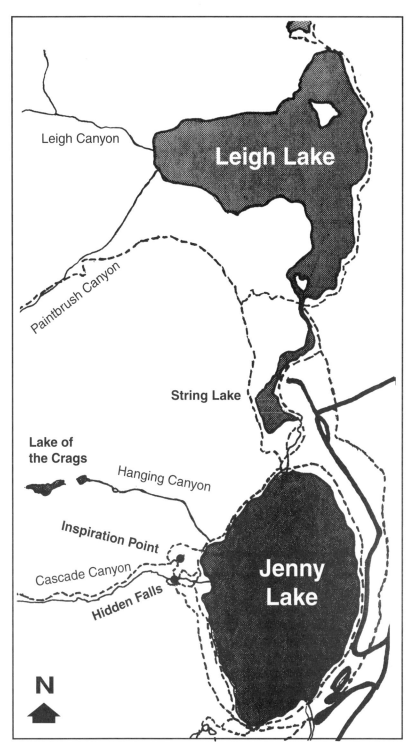

CASCADE CANYON

▲

13 HIDDEN FALLS & INSPIRATION POINT
14 FORKS OF CASCADE CANYON
15 LAKE SOLITUDE
16 HURRICANE PASS/ALASKA BASIN

Distance:
- Hidden Falls & Inspiration Point: 2.9 miles one-way
- Forks of Cascade Canyon: 6.5 miles one-way
- Lake Solitude: 9.2 miles one-way
- Hurricane Pass: 11.6 miles one-way

Elevation gain:
- Hidden Falls & Inspiration Point: 417 ft.
- Forks of Cascade Canyon: 1,057 ft.
- Lake Solitude: 2,252 ft.
- Hurricane Pass: 3,589 ft.

Maximum elevation:
- Hidden Falls & Inspiration Point: 7,200 ft.
- Forks of Cascade Canyon: 7,840 ft.
- Lake Solitude: 9,035 ft.
- Hurricane Pass: 10,372 ft.

Maps:
- Jenny Lake
- Mount Moran
- Grand Teton

Note: If starting from the west shore boat dock, deduct 2 miles from the mileages listed.

The sheer beauty and accessibility of Cascade Canyon draws more hikers than any other area in the park. The deep, U-shaped glacial canyon cuts far into the range just north of Teewinot, offering superb views of that mountain, Mt. Owen and the Grand Teton. The lower canyon is shaded by Engelmann spruce and Douglas fir, and carpeted with favorite moose browse: huckleberries and scrub willow.

From its mouth at Jenny Lake,

Hidden Falls, at the mouth of the canyon, is one of the most popular hikes in the park.

Cascade Canyon extends due west 4.5 miles before branching north towards Lake Solitude and south towards Hurricane Pass and Alaska Basin, all destinations of striking beauty. Because of its popularity the area around Lake Solitude has been closed to camping since 1972 and the number of overnight backcountry travelers in the upper forks of the canyon limited. Current camping sites are located about a mile below the lake.

To reach the trail up Cascade Canyon, drive 12 miles north of Jackson on U. S. Hwy 89/191 to Moose Junction. Turn left and drive past park headquarters and through the Moose Entrance Station. Roughly seven miles past the entrance station turn left at the South Jenny Lake Junction and park in the large lot. Follow directional signs to the boat dock, cross the bridge over Cottonwood Creek and turn left to access the trail around the north end of Jenny. Alternately, take the boat across the lake to the west shore boat dock and follow the signs to Hidden Falls and the canyon.

Hidden Falls & Inspiration Point

Both horse and people trod on the wide, heavily-used path leading to Hidden Falls and Inspiration Point. You gain elevation slowly as you climb to the top of the moraine, reaching a junction at one mile with a trail that drops down to the Moose Ponds. From the overlook the largest of the three small ponds can be clearly seen below you. The ponds often feature both moose and beaver.

Stay on the trail past the overlook and continue a slight uphill climb, entering the trees as you swing around to the west side of the lake. In another mile you reach the well-marked junction to Hidden Falls.

Turn left and follow the half mile trail as it climbs to the base of the falls, a popular spot that is truly hidden until you are almost upon it. The 200 foot plus drop thunders in early season when heavy snowmelt turns Cascade Creek into a white torrent.

To reach the trail to Inspiration Point and enter Cascade Canyon, backtrack a short distance to the bridge over Cascade Creek. Cross the bridge and follow the trail .4 miles to the well-known overlook.

The steep path has been cut through an imposing rock wall, dropping off steeply on first the right then the left side as it switchbacks its way to Inspiration Point at 7,200 feet. The point rises almost 500 feet above Jenny Lake and provides good views of the second largest lake in the park and the Gros Ventre mountains.

Forks of Cascade Canyon

Beyond Inspiration Point, the Cascade Canyon Trail continues to ascend but at a much gentler grade, gaining only 640 feet on its way to the trail junction 3.6 miles to the west. The steep north side of Mt. Owen, the second highest peak in the park at 12,928 feet, is seen to your left as you continue to ascend the lower, forested slopes of the canyon. At 3.5 miles Cascade Creek widens considerably at a spot known as Perch's Pond. This was created by rockfall from the lower slopes of Storm Point which dammed the creek. The pond is a good place to take a break and look for climbers testing their skill on Guides' Wall, the southwest ridge of Storm Point.

Numerous tributaries from the flanks of Teewinot and Mt. Owen to the south and Rock of Ages and The Jaw to the north flow into Cascade Creek as you walk up the valley. Roughly a mile before the canyon divides you'll see a thin, silvery casade tumbling down the left-hand side of the canyon. A hard scramble up either side of this stream leads to Valhalla Canyon over 2,200 feet above the creek floor. That high, hanging canyon at the base of Mt. Owen and the north side of the Grand is an ambitious goal for day hikers skilled in cross-country travel. It is quite difficult for backpackers carrying a load as it involves a tricky crossing of Cascade Creek and steep scrambling.

Cascade Creek forks .3 miles before the trail splits. Cross the bridge and continue west to the marked junction 6.5 miles from the trailhead that offers a good turn around point for those who prefer a shorter outing.

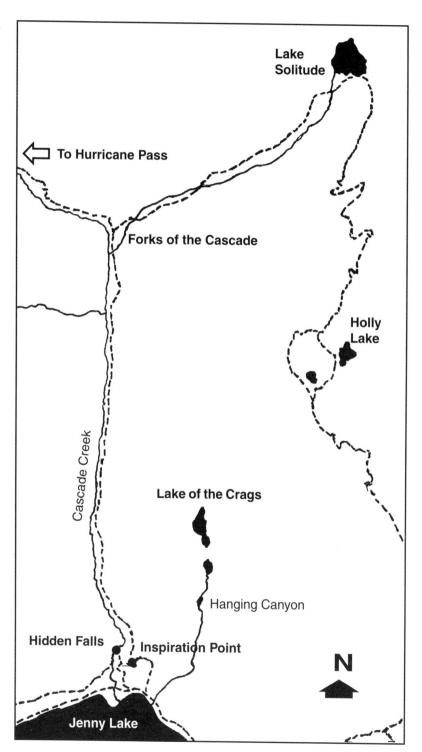

Lake Solitude

Many day hikers continue another 2.7 miles up the north fork of Cascade Canyon to reach Lake Solitude at 9,035 feet. To reach the lake, turn right at the signed trail junction and begin climbing up the forested trail. After approximately one mile you leave the trees and enter the high, grassy alpine zone. Paintbrush Divide, a 10,700 foot mountain pass, is clearly seen to your right. To your left the pointy Wigwam peaks define the skyline.

The trail gains almost 1,200 feet in under three miles. It steepens considerably just before the lake as it switchbacks up the rocky moraine around Lake Solitude. It is readily evident from the trail that horses frequent the area. Plan on treating all surface water encountered on this hike.

Lake Solitude is ringed by rocky cliffs on three sides. A scramble up the northwest side brings you to the high basin below Littles Peak and the head of South Leigh Creek, a cross-country option down the west side of the range for those interested in a multi-day trip. The north side of the lake provides an unparalleled view of Teewinot, Owen and the Grand. Framed by wildflowers in late July/early August, this is one of the most breathtaking spots in the range. But don't expect to find solitude — local hikers often sarcastically call this lovely spot "Lake Multitude."

Another popular option from Lake Solitude is to follow the trail above the North Fork of the Cascades to Paintbrush Divide, 2.4 miles beyond the lake, and return to the valley floor via Paintbrush Canyon. This is a long and strenuous route and while possible as a lengthy day trip, it is most commonly done as an overnight backpack trip.

Hurricane Pass and Alaska Basin

By turning left at the Forks of Cascade Canyon, hikers can follow the South Fork of Cascade Creek to Hurricane Pass and Alaska Basin. Not as heavily used as the North Fork Trail, the path climbs just over 2,500 feet in 5.1 miles before cresting at 10,372 feet and dropping into a rocky alpine basin on the west side of the Teton range.

Shortly past the Fork the trail begins the first of three steep switchbacks, opening up to a fine view of the steep buttresses of Table Mountain. This peak's large, flat summit gives it its name. Photographer William Jackson took the first pictures of the Grand Teton from Table's summit in 1872.

Roughly a mile beyond Table Mountain the path enters a forest of impressive whitebark pine trees, many larger than five feet in diameter. It passes through this magnificent stand of trees for the next two miles before reaching treeline 10 miles from the start of the trail.

Four short but steep switchbacks lead to a trail junction at 10.3 miles. The left trail leads to Avalanche Canyon Divide. The Park Service abandoned that trail because rockfall at the base of The Wall — the limestone cliffbands to the south — rendered it unsafe. Hikers are advised to not travel on this trail.

The trail over high, wind-swept Hurricane Pass drops into scenic Alaska Basin on the west side of the Teton Range.

Take the right fork of the trail and climb the switchbacks through the talus 1.3 miles to the top of Hurricane Pass, passing above Schoolroom Glacier to your left (S). Of the 14 glaciers in Grand Teton National Park, this permanent snowfield is marked by textbook examples of lateral and terminal moraines, crevasses, and a lake clouded by glacial flour (powdered rock) at its toe; thus, its name.

The trail tops out at 10,372 foot Hurricane Pass, supplying sweeping views of the Grand, Middle and South Tetons, Avalanche Divide, and The Wall. From here it drops steeply west into rock-studded Alaska Basin and Sunset Lake 2.7 miles below.

Guide Paul Petzoldt named the basin in 1924 after he and a horse party crossed the snow-covered alpine meadows early in the season. Its beauty and accessibility from both sides of the range has led to heavy use of the area, particularly since Targhee National Forest presently does not require overnight permits to camp in the basin.

Backpackers seeking solitude would be wise to secure a permit from the park to camp in the upper reaches of the South Fork instead of near the lake.

▲

17 HANGING CANYON

Distance:
  String Lake to Lake of the Crags: 7 miles RT
  West Shore Dock to Lake of the Crags: 4 miles RT
Elevation gain:
  2,690 ft.
Maximum elevation:
  9565 ft.
Maps:
  Jenny Lake
  Mount Moran

Surrounded on all but the east side by towering pinnacles, and virtually hidden from the valley below, this magnificent canyon leads to an impressive cirque and a trio of lakes. The view from the highest, Lake of the Crags, is one of the most dramatic vistas in the Tetons, in many ways surpassing the beauty of the signature peaks for which the range is known.

While the canyon does not have an official trail many hikers, as well as climbers heading to Cube Point, Symmetry Spire, The Jaw and other destinations, have worn a path to the lakes. The trail is extremely steep — gaining almost 2,700 feet in under two miles — and involves both route finding and scrambling to reach the upper lakes. Hanging Canyon is not a good choice for inexperienced hikers or young children.

The most common approach to the canyon is via the west shore boat dock on Jenny Lake. Drive 12 miles north of Jackson of U.S. Hwy 89/191 to the Moose Junction. Turn left, pass park headquarters and go through the Moose Entrance station into Grand Teton National Park. Follow the park road for seven miles to the signed South Jenny Lake Junction. Turn left at the junction and follow the signs to the boat dock. During the summer months Teton Boating Co. ferries customers across the lake for a small fee, operating continuously from 8 a.m. to 6 p.m. The trip across the lake takes about 20 minutes and saves 1.5 miles each way.

Turn right off the west shore boat dock and walk northwest roughly one-quarter of a mile. You'll cross two bridges that span a marshy area and Hanging Canyon Creek tumbling down from the canyon above you. Pass the horse trail turn-off up Cascade Canyon. Shortly after the second bridge an unmarked path heads left (W) through the trees. Turn here to start hiking up Hanging Canyon.

Alternately, one can continue driving past the South Jenny Lake Junction to signs marking the North Jenny Lake Junction and String Lake. Turn left here and drive to the String Lake turn-off. Park at the first parking area at String Lake and cross the hiker's

Rock of Ages, seen above Lake of the Crags in Hanging Canyon.

bridge near the outlet. Turn left at the String Lake/Jenny Lake trail junction and walk along the west side of the creek then southwest along the shore of Jenny Lake until you see the unmarked trail on your right. I prefer this option: it warms up your legs and lungs for the climb, avoids the crowds at the boat dock and allows you to spend the boat fare on a beer at Dornan's when you return.

The trail up Hanging Canyon ascends the east flank of Mount St. John, staying on the right (N) side of Hanging Canyon Creek. It winds steeply up through pines and open slopes on the lower section to rock slabs above. To help prevent further erosion of the steep slopes, stay on the unofficial trail/route marked by cairns.

Shortly before you reach Arrowhead Pool the trail swings close to Ribbon Cascades. Monkshood, forget-me-nots and columbine thrive in the mid-summer mountain run-off, making this a beautiful place for a rest stop. Parties interested in scrambling up Cube Point, the 9,000 plus foot peak at the end of Symmetry Spire's east ridge, should cross the stream here and head left (S) to its base. To continue on to Ramshead Lake and Lake of the Crags, stay on the right side of the stream and follow the cairns. The route ends in the talus slopes on the west side of Ramshead. A short scramble up and over these brings you to the head of the canyon and the final lake.

And what a spot it is! This alpine jewel is surrounded by jagged, perpendicular peaks and pinnacles. The impressive flat-topped peak to the southwest is Rock of Ages, so named because it is "good" climbing rock. Ayres' Crags extend from the Rock northward to The Jaw (11,400 feet), the highest pinnacle due west. Mount St. John dominates the northern skyline.

Hikers with sufficient mountaineering skill may want to consider scrambling up the non-technical east face of The Jaw by following the canyon's western benches and talus slopes to the summit. The summit offers impressive views of the north and northwest faces of Teewinot, Mt. Owen and the Grand Teton.

There is space for a party of two to camp near the trees on Lake of the Crags' north shore. Much more desirable sites, however, are located due east of Ramshead Lake in the 1934 burn area, where charred trees still mark the site of the lightning strike.

▲

18 HOLLY LAKE & PAINTBRUSH DIVIDE

Distance:
    Holly Lake:12.4 miles RT
    Paintbrush Divide: 7.9 miles one-way
Elevation gain:
    Holly Lake: 2,535 ft.
    Paintbrush Divide: 3,835 ft.
Maximum elevation:
    9,410 ft.
Maps:
    Jenny Lake
    Mount Moran

Holly Lake lies at the bottom of a glacial cirque below 11,590 foot Mount Woodring. The pretty lake is reached by a steep trail up Paintbrush Canyon through both coniferous forest and rocky terrain. It switchbacks up three distinct glacial benches as it gains over 2,500 feet on its way to the lake. Striking views of the north side of Rockchuck Peak and permanent snowfields beneath The Jaw and Mount St. John, as well as the fiery red flowers that give the canyon its name, lend to this hike's popularity.

For a description of how to reach the trailhead and the first 1.7 miles of trail, please refer to Hike No. 11 around String Lake.

At the String Lake/Paintbrush Canyon trail junction turn right and begin walking northwest through dense coniferous forest. The trail bears steadily west through the forested slopes of lower Paintbrush Canyon until it reaches Paintbrush Canyon Creek, roughly 3.2 miles and almost a thousand feet above the trailhead. The trail soon crosses a bridge over the creek and follows the creek's north side through scattered trees and rocky slopes. After numerous small crossings of side streams tumbling down Rockchuck, Mount Woodring and Mount St. John's above you, you'll ascend several wooded switchbacks before heading due west up a long, straight stretch to a trail junction at 5.7 miles. The left trail leads to the camping zone below Paintbrush Divide. Take the right trail and ascend two short, steep switchbacks before crossing the outlet to a small lake on your left This is not Holly Lake, which lies another .3 miles further up the trail.

Holly lake is a perfect spot to enjoy lunch before heading back down. Around it rise the rocky slopes of Mount Woodring. Looking down the canyon from the lake, the permanent snowfields and sheer north side of The Jaw dominate the view to the right, while the valley floor can be seen far below.

A return via the same route makes a nice, if long, day. Those skilled in off-trail, cross-country travel could ascend the small saddle northwest of the lake and drop into Grizzly Bear Lake in upper Leigh Canyon. Walk down that trailless canyon to the west shore of Leigh Lake, then String Lake. This is a beautiful, rugged trip of several days duration.

Paintbrush Divide

Alternatively, you could continue west on the trail past the lake and rejoin the main trail to Paintbrush Divide, reached 1.7 miles and 1,300 feet above Holly Lake.

From the divide the trail drops into the upper reaches of the North Fork of Cascade Canyon to Lake Solitude. It then descends Cascade Canyon to Jenny Lake. This is one of the most popular backpacking trips in the park. While it is occasionally done as a long day hike, taking two or three days is much more popular and enjoyable. Due to heavy use Holly Lake and Lake Solitude have been closed to camping since 1972. Camping is permitted in zones below both lakes.

Holly Lake is named after Holly Leek, the daughter of one of the valley's earliest residents, rancher Stephen Leek. Leek's photographs of elk starving during severe Jackson Hole winters were instrumental in establishing the National Elk Refuge north of Jackson.

The upper reaches of Paintbrush Canyon near Holly Lake.

19 SCHWABACHER'S LANDING

Distance:
 Varies. Not more than 4.5 miles RT
Elevation gain:
 Negligible
Map:
 None needed

Schwabacher's Landing is a popular launch site for rafters and anglers. It also draws interest from those on foot. Fishing along the banks of the Snake River attracts wader-clad piscators from April 1 to October 31. The skillful may keep up to six fish a day; one may be over 18 inches. Everything between 11-18 inches must be released immediately. Complete rules and regulations are given to anglers when they buy a required Wyoming license.

Amateur and professional photographers stalk not the wily trout, but the perfect shot. Most of the famed pictures of the Tetons reflected in a still body of water are shot at dawn or dusk along the river's quiet side channels. That same peaceful environment is home to beaver, moose, elk, otter, eagles and waterfowl—wildlife commonly seen by visitors to the riverbank. In the fall, elk bugle poignantly as they crash through the cottonwoods seeking hormonal relief.

The landing is easily accessed by driving north out of Jackson on U.S. Hwy. 89/191. Pass Moose Junction at 12 miles, continuing north another four miles to the signed Schwabacher Landing Road on your left. Turn in. The steep gravel road divides in .6 miles. The left fork leads to a parking area. The right travels north another .4 miles to the lower landing. Either one is a fine jumping-off point. The first parking area is the most popular starting point for hikers.

With the river on one side and the road on the other, it is difficult to get lost. Wander at will, but exercise caution if you decide to step into the river. The current is often stronger than it appears.

Schwabacher Landing

20 HERMITAGE POINT
21 LAKESHORE TRAIL

Distance:
   Hermitage Point: 9.5 miles RT
   Lakeshore Trail: 1.8 miles RT
Elevation gain:
   Negligible
Maximum elevation:
   Approximately 8,000 ft.

Maps:
   Colter Bay

The sagebrush meadows, lodgepole pine forests, thick willows and marshy areas along Jackson Lake's eastern shoreline near Colter Bay provide ideal habitat for wildlife. Muskrat, otter, and beaver thrive in the still inlets. Moose and elk often browse on the plentiful vegetation, while cranes, ducks and trumpeter swans set up housekeeping in the same. Nature's inhabitants are most active in the soft light of dawn and dusk, when reflections of the Grand and Mt. Moran color Jackson Lake with delicate shades of gold, rose and peach.

A number of trials criss-cross this peaceful area. All are virtually flat, climbing only small rises as they follow the lakeshore. The trail network offers several possibilities: two are presented below. To reach the area, drive north out of Jackson 30 miles on U.S. Hwy. 89/191 to Moran Junction. Turn left unto U.S. Hwy 89/287 and drive 10 miles to the Colter Bay turn-off on the left-hand side of the road, passing the turn-off to Jackson Lake Lodge. The trail to Hermitage Point starts at the southeast end of the visitor center's parking lot. The Lakeshore Trail starts behind the visitor's center.

Hermitage Point

From the trailhead walk right through flat, sagebrush covered terrain towards an inlet of Jackson Lake. The trail closely parallels the lake's eastern shore until you reach a junction at .4 miles. Take the left fork, turning away from Jackson Lake and walking southeast towards Swan Lake, a long, shallow body of water that is home to trumpeter swans and other nesting waterfowl. Be sure to bring your binoculars so you can observe the birds without disturbing their nesting activity.

At 1.7 miles the trail forks again. The right fork leads to Heron Pond, then back to the trailhead. This makes a nice three-mile loop for those interested in a shorter hike. To reach Hermitage Point, take the left fork and continue walking around the southern end of Swan Lake for another half-mile to the outlet of Third Creek. Here the trail splits again. Take the right fork, passing through thickets of willow and marshland as you follow Third Creek down its short course to Jackson Lake. Elk and moose are often seen along this section of the trail, drawn by the rich grasses and tasty willow branches.

At 2.9 miles the trail divides yet again, the right fork looping back to the trailhead along the eastern shore of Jackson Lake. Take the left-hand trail and walk through lodgepole pine trees and sagebrush flats for 2.2 miles to the end of Hermitage Point, a nice place to enjoy the great view and reflections of the Grand Teton and Mt. Moran when Jackson Lake is calm.

The peninsula was named Hermitage Point because of a developer's plans to build an inn, or hermitage, there. After procuring a large quantity of logs for the project the developer scotched the idea. He floated the logs down the Snake and sold them off. While the lodge was never built, the point retained its name.

From the end of the peninsula the trail swings north and follows the lake's eastern shore for three miles, reaching a junction near Heron Pond at 8.1 miles. Take the trail to the left, paralleling the pond, to return to the trailhead in another 1.4 miles, for a total of 9.5 miles.

Lakeshore Trail

The blacktop trail that starts near the visitors' center leads to a causeway to the small island in front of the center. The short but worthwhile Lakeshore Trail circles this island. An interpretative brochure of this and other Col-

Square-topped Mount Moran is clearly seen from the trail to Hermitage Point.

ter Bay trails is available at the visitor's center, and is well worth its modest cost. In addition to wonderful views of the Tetons at the west end of the island, hikers can clearly see the effects of forest fire. Look for evidence of 1932 and 1974 burns near the mouths of Moran and Waterfall Canyons across the lake.

From the visitor center, walk north of the marina on a paved walk for approximately .3 miles. Here, you'll cross the causeway to the island. The mostly forested trail circles it. Near the island's west end, the trail dips to the lakeshore, where you enjoy fine view of the Tetons.

The island juts into part of Colter Bay, a shallow harbor formed in 1916 when completion of a dam at the south end of Jackson Lake raised the lake's water level over nine feet. When the lake level was lowered in the mid-1980s to repair and rebuilt the old dam, archeologists unearthed interesting Indian artifacts.

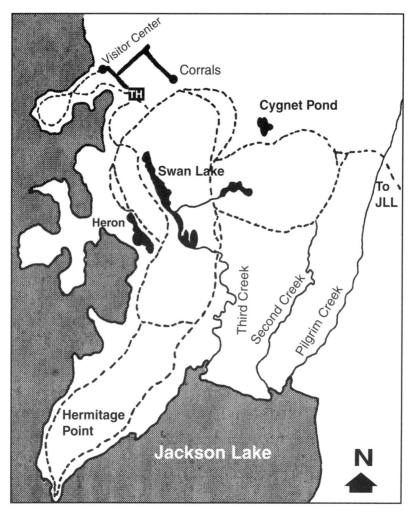

22 JLL TO COLTER BAY

Distance:
    4.5 miles one-way
Elevation gain:
    Negligible
Maximum elevation:
    Approx. 6,800 ft.
Maps:
    See adjacent page

An often overlooked but pleasant trail is the old roadbed between Jackson Lake Lodge and Colter Bay. This flat, 4.5 mile one-way hike may be started from Willows Flats Overlook, or, as described here, from an asphalt walk at the south end of Jackson Lake Lodge. It ends at the horse corrals at Colter Bay. In addition to views of Jackson Lake and the Teton Range north of the Grand, hikers enjoy a panoply of wildlife and forest environments enroute. Both are wonderfully described in an inexpensive trail pamphlet published by the Grand Teton Natural History Association, available for purchase in the lodge.

To reach the lodge and trailhead, drive 30 miles north of Jackson on U.S. Hwy. 89/1291 to Moran Junction. Turn left unto U.S. Hwy. 89/287 and drive through the Buffalo Entrance Station to Grand Teton National Park. Four miles north of the entrance, drive straight past the turn-off to Jackson Lake and Signal Mountain. It is another .8 miles to the well-signed turn-off to Jackson Lake Lodge on your left. Park in the back lot and walk to the south end of the lodge (left of the building's main entrance) to a paved asphalt trail that quickly drops to the old road.

The road/trail cuts through Willow Flats, the name given to the large freshwater marsh sandwiched between the lodge and Jackson Lake. Here, the ponds, willows and small grassy openings provide ideal protection and food for beaver, moose, elk, cranes and a host of winged friends—including yellow-headed blackbirds, sparrows, barn swallows, flycatchers, woodpeckers and soras. It is a nice area to sit and simply observe the critters.

As you walk north beyond Willow Flats, the road travels through stands of spruce and fir before crossing a bridge over Pilgrim Creek at 1.8 miles. Shortly after the bridge the terrain opens up to reveal views of Mount Moran framed by conifers and stately cottonwoods. This section is spectacular in fall, when the trees are dressed in gold and the low-angle light paints the silhouettes of the jagged Tetons soldier blue. It's a satisfying area to eat lunch off-trail.

A junction is reached at 2.4 miles.

55

The triangle of trails in this vicinity is a bit confusing, made worse by poorly placed Park Service signage. Stay right to continue on to Colter Bay, left to reach Second Creek and/or Hermitage Point. The trail to Colter Bay skirts the south side of Cygnet Pond, where I've often seen moose browsing.

At 3.6 miles, you'll reach a second junction. Two routes here lead to Colter Bay. The shorter one, .8 miles in length, goes past the sewage holding ponds to reach the corrals. The longer option at 1.2 miles travels east of the ponds.

If you have shuttled a car in advance, your hike is done at the corrals. A number of longer loop hikes are also possible. Consult the map.

▲

23 CHRISTIAN POND

Distance:
    3.3 miles RT
Elevation gain:
    240 ft.
Maximum elevation:
    6,440 ft.
Maps:
    Moran
    Two Ocean Lake

The short walk around Christian Pond offers some of the best opportunities in the valley to view trumpeter swans, a rainbow palette of wildflowers, and views of the Tetons—without lung-searing or knee-busting climbs and drops. Not surprisingly the trail receives a fair amount of use, including horse traffic from Jackson Lake Lodge. If you begin before 8 a.m., however, you'll most likely have this delightful walk to yourself.

The trail begins near the horse corrals at Jackson Lake Lodge, reached by driving north of Jackson on U.S. Hwy. 89/191. You may either turn left at Moose Junction and take the inner park road to its junction with U.S. Hwy. 89/287—turning left there to reach the lodge—or continue straight and drive another 18 miles to Moran Junction. Turn left, pass through the Buffalo Entrance Station, then drive another 4 miles north to the signed turn-off. The second alternative is longer (35 vs. 30 miles from Jackson), but is often quicker in the summer since the inner park road tends to draw more traffic.

From the corrals, the trail passes

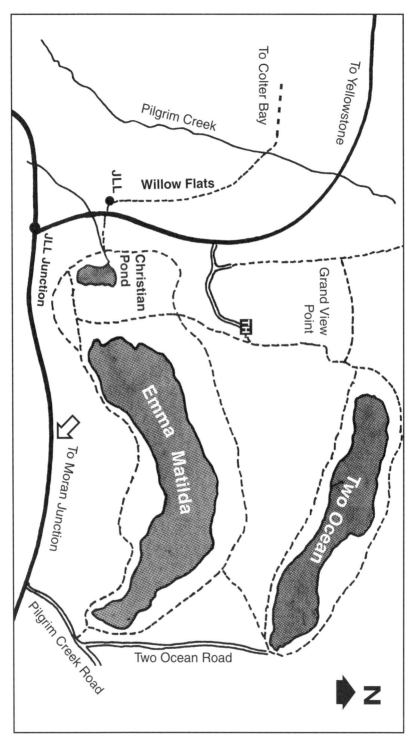

under a highway bridge spanning Christian Creek and climbs a small knoll to a signed trail junction. Either direction takes you around Christian Pond. For purpose of description, turn right. The trail travels through a marshy section before ascending an overlook above the pond. This is a superb place to view waterfowl, particularly a pair of nesting trumpeter swans. Please do not leave the trail for a closer look: you may disturb their nest site. Bring a pair of binoculars to observe the swans, coots, teals, yellow-headed blackbirds and splashy blue-billed ruddy ducks.

Beyond the overlook, the trail parallels the west side of the pond, reaching a junction at the one mile mark. The right fork leads towards a nature trail through Oxbow Bend Go left here, and again at 1.2 miles, where the trail splits to circumnavigate Emma Matilda Lake. This section of the hike climbs at an easy grade through huge Douglas fir, Engelmann spruce and aspen glades to a ridge, an elevation gain that unveils views of the pond, Jackson Lake and the Tetons. The trail then descends to another junction at 2.2 miles. Keep to the left to return to the horse corrals. The trail drops then levels as it travels through willowed lowland. After turning west it ascends the short distance to the corrals.

Christian Pond and creek were named after Charles A. "Tex" Christian, who managed one of the first lodges in the area.

▲

24 EMMA MATILDA LAKE

Distance:
    11 miles RT
Elevation gain:
    Approx. 550 ft.
Elevation loss:
    Approx. 380 ft.
Maximum elevation:
    7,320 ft.
    Two Ocean

The trail around Emma Matilda Lake climbs several hundred feet to a ridge above its north shore, a vantage point that provides panoramic views of Jackson Lake and the Tetons to the west. It tempts fewer hikers than other park trails, perhaps because of its length and recent history of bear sightings. Travel with companions and make noise should you choose to walk around this pretty lake.

Driving directions and the first 2.2

miles of trail are described in the Christian Pond hike on page 57. At the 2.2 mile junction, the trail to Emma Matilda turns right (NE) and ascends 320 feet to a ridge above the north side of the lake. The long, crescent shaped body of water is cradled between two ridges. It rests almost 100 feet higher than Jackson Lake, seen in the distance to the west.

The trail travels the length of the ridge, then gradually drops to an intersection with a trail leading to Two Ocean Lake at 4.7 miles. Stay right here to continue around Emma Matilda. The trail bends south around the lake's east end, staying 100 feet above it until it descends to cross a footbridge over its outlet at 6.6 miles. (You will pass two spur trails enroute. These lead to an access road to the lakes off Pacific Creek Road. Stay right at both of these junctions.)

Beyond the footbridge, the trail hugs the lakeshore for over a mile then gently climbs almost 200 feet above it through thick forest. It veers close to the shore again at 8.4 miles, traversing southwest through fir and stately Englemann spruce. Stay right at 8.8 miles and again at 9.4 miles, where trails lead south to the Oxbow Bend area.

At 9.8 miles, the Emma Matilda Trail rejoins the trail around Christian Pond. Go left at this junction, retracing the first 1.2 miles of the hike to return to your vehicle.

The lake is named Emma Matilda after William Owen's wife. She unsuccessfully attempted to climb the Grand Teton with him in 1891. He did successfully scale the peak seven years later. Although some controversy exists in regards to the Grand's mountaineering history, many believe Owen's climb was the first ascent of the peak.

It is not unusual to see elk at dawn or dusk on the Emma Matilda hike.

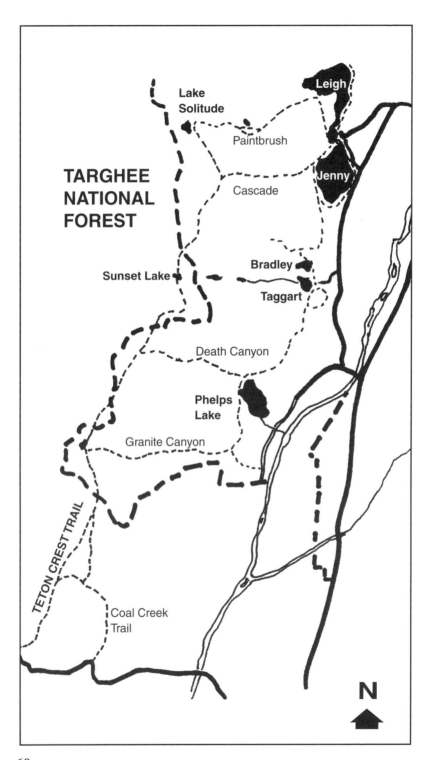

25 TETON CREST TRAIL

Distance:
    Teton Pass to Moose Creek Divide: 7.2 miles
    Moose Creek Divide to Fox Creek Pass: 5 miles
    Fox Creek Pass to Basin Lakes: 5.7 miles
    Basin Lakes to Hurricane Pass: 2.6 miles
    Hurricane Pass to Forks of Cascade Canyon: 5.1 miles
    Forks of Cascade Canyon to Paintbrush Divide: 5.1 miles
    Paintbrush Divide to String Lake Parking Area: 7.9 miles
        Total distance: 38.6 miles

Elevation gained:
    Teton Pass to Moose Creek Divide: 1,285 ft.
    Moose Creek Divide to Fox Creek Pass: 520 ft.
    Fox Creek Pass to Basin Lakes: -40 ft.
    Basin Lakes to Hurricane Pass: 812 ft.
    Hurricane Pass to Forks of Cascade: -2,532. ft
    Forks of Cascade Canyon to Paintbrush Divide: 2,880 ft.
    Paintbrush Divide to String Lake Parking area: -3,845 ft.

Maximum elevation:
    Paintbrush Divide: 10,720 ft.

Maps:
    Teton Pass
    Rendezvous Peak
    Mount Bannon
    Grand Teton
    Mount Moran
    Jenny Lake

    The Teton Crest Trail runs along the spine of the range, beginning at Moose Creek Divide at the park's southern boundary and heading north to Hurricane Pass at the head of the South Fork of Cascade Canyon. By walking up either Coal Creek Canyon or Phillips Pass to reach Moose Creek Divide, hiking the central portion, and then walking from Hurricane Pass to Paintbrush Divide and down the canyon of the same name, you complete one of the most spectacular mountain walks in the entire United States. The almost 40 mile trail weaves in-and-out of Grand Teton National Park and the Jedediah Smith Wilderness Area of Targhee National Forest as it crosses from the west to the east side of the range. It skirts dozens of small alpine lakes, traverses the dramatic Death Canyon Shelf, and crosses five passes or divides along its course. Wildflowers are plentiful from mid-

July to mid-August, and the chance of seeing moose, mountain sheep and possibly black bears is good.

The time the trip takes depends on personal preference. Fit and speedy souls can blitz it in as little as two long days. Those with lots of time, who enjoy dallying in beautiful camping spots or striking out on side trips, might easily spend more than a week on the trail. In general, four nights and five days will allow a comfortable pace of seven miles a day (remember, you're at high altitude and carrying weight on your back).

As many segments of this trail are described elsewhere in this book, the description below is given for general directions only. Please consult individual write-ups for more detail. The elevation gains listed in the information capsule record only the difference between the starting and ending point and do not register drops and subsequent gains along the way.

You may begin the trail by hiking up Coal Creek Canyon and over Mesquite Pass to reach Moose Creek Divide, or from the eastern side of Teton Pass to Phillips Pass and the Divide. The latter is slightly shorter, and since you are starting at a higher elevation on the Pass, it saves you about 500 feet of initial ascent.

From 9,085 foot Moose Creek Divide, the Crest Trail drops to the junction with the Middle Fork Cutoff Trail to your right, 7.8 miles from the start of the trail's southern end.

This area is a good place to begin looking for a camp spot for the first evening as the high meadows offer a nice view, water from intermittent streams, lots of wildflowers and a good chance of spotting moose and deer at dawn and dusk.

From the Middle Fork Cutoff, the trail follows a 2.7 mile up-and-down course to Marion Lake, skirts its east side and then begins climbing up a steep slope towards a high bench and 9,600 foot Fox Creek Pass, 2.3 miles beyond the lake. From there it heads north, dropping onto the relatively level Death Canyon Shelf. This 3.5 mile long limestone bench drops off abruptly to the east into Death Canyon. Above it to the west tower four peaks over 10,600 feet: Fossil Mountain, Mount Bannon, Mount Jedediah Smith, and Mount Meek.

The shelf is a classic example of Karst topography. Slightly acidic rainwater has eaten through cracks and crevices of the soft dolomite and limestone rock, forming underground passages and caverns. It is one of the prettiest places in the Tetons and an excellent place to camp. A spot near the bench's northern end is a good stopping point for the second evening.

From the northern end of Death Canyon Shelf, the Crest trail climbs over 9,726 foot Mount Meek Pass and leaves Grand Teton National Park before descending to Basin Lakes in the Jedediah Smith Wilderness Area of Targhee National Forest, 17.9 miles from the start of the trail. Passing a cluster of eight lakes, it steeply gains elevation as it climbs towards 10,382 foot Hurricane Pass 2.6 miles to the north.

Dropping off the pass back into Grand Teton National Park, the trail passes Schoolroom Glacier and descends the South Fork of Cascade Canyon. The South Fork features an impressive forest of whitebark pine, some estimated to be over 400 years

Distinctive Battleship Mountain is framed by fields of wildflowers.

old. Here one gets wonderful views of the west side of the Middle and Grand Tetons. The northern, lower reaches of the South Fork is a good place to camp for the third evening.

The trail drops from the South Fork of Cascade Canyon to the Forks, 25.6 miles from the start of your trip. Go left at the Forks (N) towards Lake Solitude. A steady climb takes you past the lake and over 10,720 foot Paintbrush Divide. This 5.1 mile segment gains 2,880 feet and brings you to the high point of the trip.

From the top of the Divide, the trail drops very steeply into upper Paintbrush Canyon. Camp for the night in the marked upper camping zone. Other sites may be found near Holly Lake, 1.7 miles below the Divide and 32.4 miles from the start of the trail.

From here your last day is an easy cruise down Paintbrush Canyon to the String Lake Parking area, a pretty downhill walk over numerous glacial benches that offer good views of Jackson, Leigh and String Lakes below you.

The Crest Trail can, of course, be walked in either direction. The main advantage of walking south to north is a more gradual start. As you head north, the hiking becomes more rugged and the scenery intensifies. Conversely, going from north to south lets one deal with the most strenuous sections early in the trip.

Granite, Death and Cascade Canyons to the east and Teton Canyon to the west all provide conveniently spaced exit routes along the course of the hike. These offer several options for shorter variations of this classic trip. But if time is available, the entire trail is highly recommended. Numerous side trips enroute are also encouraged.

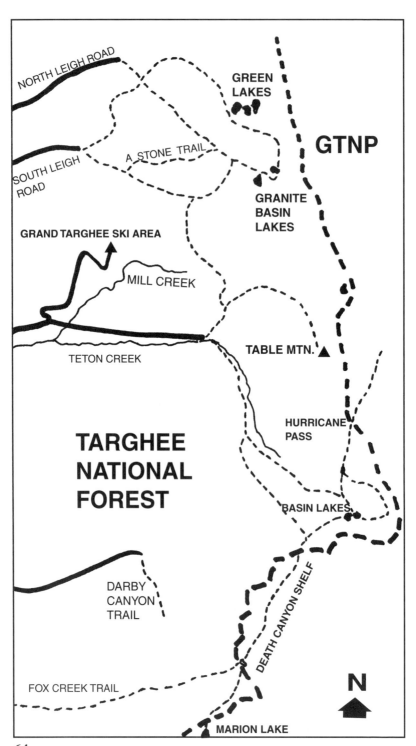

The West Slope

▲

When Grand Teton National Park was established in 1929 park boundaries ended at the crest of the range. The gentler, western slopes of the range were already part of Targhee National Forest, established 21 years earlier. Targhee's 1.7 million acres extend north to Yellowstone National Park, east to Grand Teton National Park, and south to the Snake River Valley in eastern Idaho, forming a huge half-circle around the Snake's headwaters.

The forest's name is shared by a pass, peak and creek. It is commonly agreed that Targhee was an Indian warrior or chief greatly admired and revered by his tribe. Beyond that the consensus disintegrates. Some accounts postulate that Targhee was a Nez Perce warrior killed the summer of 1877 in a battle between Chief Joseph and the U.S. Cavalry near Henry's Lake, Idaho. Chief Joseph was reportedly skirmishing with the army in an attempt to buy time for the remainder of his beleaguered Nez Perce tribe fleeing northward to Canada. Other stories, however, state that Targhee was not a Nez Perce, but a Shoshone Indian, killed during a battle with the Crow Indians the winter of 1871. Whichever tribe he belonged to, Targhee's name remains as a testament to his courage.

Within Targhee National Forest lies the 116,535 acre Jedediah Smith Wilderness Area. This encompasses the west slope of the Tetons and all of the hikes outlined in this section. Like his counterpart Jim Bridger, this famous mountain man made his living trapping fur in the region near the turn of the century. The wilderness is named in his honor.

The base of the western slope is generally characterized by thick forests of aspen, lodgepole pine, Douglas fir, Engelmann spruce and verdant meadows colored by spectacular wildflowers. The lush flora is nourished by over four feet of annual rainfall, making the west slope of the range the garden spot of the predominantly dry, sage-covered Cowboy State.

Starting at a higher average base elevation, the grade of the western canyons is not as steep as those on the eastern side of the range. Most of the canyons are wide, U-shaped passages between surrounding peaks and ridges that crest and drop abruptly into the east side of the range. Ascending them provides views not only of the cirques and high alpine lakes at their head, but the upper reaches of the eastern canyons and the craggy Tetons as well. Instead of looking down to the valley floor, hikers on the west slope look directly at the Tetons themselves. Geologically this side is different too. While the famous east side of the Teton Range is composed primarily of granitic gneiss, the west side features vast, gently sloping limestone shelves hundreds of feet thick, many of which are riddled with caves.

Over 1,200 miles of trail criss-cross Targhee National Forest and the west slope. It is not uncommon for trails to be snowbound well into July, particularly following a wet, snowy spring. Check on current trail conditions by calling the Teton Basin Ranger District of Targhee National Forest at (208)-354-2431, or write:

>Targhee National Forest
>Teton Basin Ranger District
>Driggs, Idaho 83422.

If you are calling on the weekend or after working hours, a taped report summarizing conditions on the forest is available by dialing 208-624-4575. Hikers using the wilderness area should acquaint themselves with the rules and regulations protecting this resource. These are outlined in a Jedediah Smith Wilderness area map available from the above address, and are also usually posted at major trailheads.

Lusher and less crowded than the more popular eastern side of the Tetons, many Jackson Holer's prefer to spend their time in the mountains on the "Idaho" side of the range, sharing the backcountry with resident moose, deer and elk rather than scores of hikers. Not as suited to the mountaineering for which the Tetons are famous, it has much greater potential for the wilderness backpacker.

Access to the west side of the range begins in the vicinity of Victor and Driggs, Idaho towns 45 minutes to one hour from Jackson via Teton Pass.

26 COAL CREEK & TAYLOR MTN.

Distance:
    7.2 miles RT
Elevation gain:
    2,788 ft.
Maximum elevation:
    10, 068 ft.
Maps:
    Rendezvous Peak

A well-maintained but not heavily used trail, alpine meadows sprinkled with wildflowers, and a summit that commands one of the finest views in the southern Tetons make Coal Creek/ Taylor Mountain an attractive choice — if you don't mind breathing hard. From the parking area to the summit, you gain almost 2,800 feet in under four miles.

The trailhead is located at the foot of Teton Pass on the ""Idaho side" of the range (Coal Creek is actually in Wyoming). Drive south of downtown Jackson on U.S. Hwy 89/191 to the junction with Wyoming Hwy. 22. Turn right and drive seven miles to Wilson, located at the base of the pass. The road gains 2,200 feet in the next 5.5 miles, cresting at an elevation of 8,431 feet. There is ample parking at the top if you wish to pull over and enjoy a view of the valley.

Drive down the west side of the pass. At the bottom you will see a well-marked turn-out for Coal Creek on the right-hand side of the road. Park and begin hiking up the signed jeep trail heading north. Cross a log bridge spanning Coal Creek and follow the well-worn path . It crosses and recrosses the creek three times before the creek forks at two miles. There are no maintained bridges, although you can often find a log across the creek.

At the fork, the trail leaves the stream and climbs steeply up an open slope and aspen groves before leveling in a grassy meadow at 2.2 miles. Watered by Coal Creek, the lush meadow often appeals to overnight campers.

The trail traverses the length of it, climbing north towards Mesquite Creek Divide, a 9,197 foot saddle that leads north to Moose Meadows.

Just before reaching the Divide at 2.6 miles, a signed trail to Taylor Mountain turns off to the left (W). That dirt and rock path gains almost a thousand feet as it climbs the additional one mile to Taylor's 10,068 foot summit. The panoramic view on top takes in the southern end of the Tetons, the Wyoming Range, and the patchwork farmlands and distant mountain ranges of Idaho.

For those preferring a longer hike several options are available from the summit. One is to follow the trail down the west side of Taylor Mountain and drop into Taylor Basin. It is

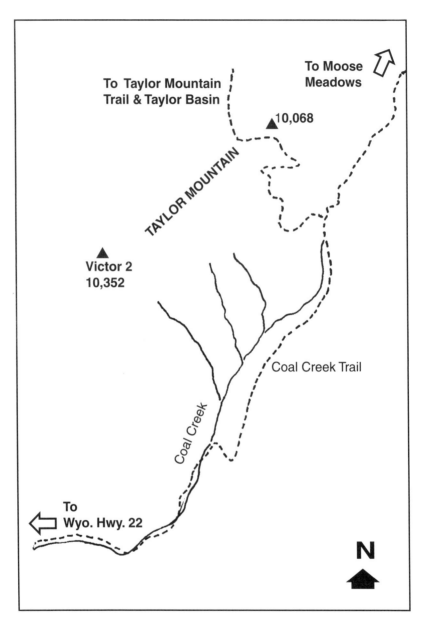

6.5 miles from Taylor's summit to Nordwall Campground at trail's end, approximately three miles southeast of Victor, Idaho. Shuttle a car before you leave or arrange to have someone pick you up.

Other options include returning to Mesquite Creek Divide and walking north towards Moose Creek, or bearing right onto a ridge that eventually leads to Phillips Pass and returning via Phillips Canyon.

Both options require map and compass skills.

27 MOOSE CREEK

Distance:
    Moose Lake: 15.8 miles RT
    Moose Creek Divide: 14 miles RT
Elevation gained:
    Moose Lake: 2,910 ft.
    Moose Creek Divide: 2,695 ft.
Maximum elevation:
    Moose Lake: 9,300 ft.
    Moose Creek Divide: 9,085 ft.
Maps:
    Victor
    Rendezvous Peak

A group of eight appealing lakes at the head of the canyon and a double waterfall are the attrractions of the Moose Creek hike. The detractions are unbridged creek crossings and heavy horse traffic that has created man-eating bogs on several sections of trail. Wet, muddy feet are a given if you select this route.

To reach the trailhead, drive from Jackson over Teton Pass to a marked Forest Service Road to Moose Creek on the right, roughly a quarter of a mile down the road from the Mike Harris Campground turn-off. The trailhead is at the end of this potholed, poorly maintained 3.3 mile road. Stay to the right at the fork, passing Nordwall Campground and continue up the road to Bear Canyon. As the last half-mile of road is usually impassable, it is a good idea to park here and walk to the trailhead.

The trail follows an old road that parallels Moose Creek, eventually narrowing as you walk up the canyon. You cross numerous tributaries as you maintain a moderate grade through forest, meadows and wide, boggy areas. The latter are good spots to watch for both moose and evidence of beaver activity. At roughly four miles you reach a trail junction at the edge of Moose Meadows. The right fork leads over Mesquite Pass to Coal Creek Canyon. Stay left, skirting the west side of the boggy field. Cross Moose Creek at the far end and begin climbing more steeply towards the head of the canyon. To your left, the 10,000 foot cliff walls that surround Moose Lake soar above tree line. A mile further the steep cirque on the backside of 10,927 foot Rendezvous Peak comes into view to your right.

At 5.7 miles the trail jogs sharply south for a short distance. At the turn, leave the trail and head left (NW) around the slope. You'll shortly walk around to a view of two large waterfalls, one of top of the other. The falls flow through a notch between two cliff bands, which the trail crosses up above. Many people walk right by them, not knowing they are there.

Backtrack to the trail, which leads south a short distance then turns northeast left (NE) and climbs 200 feet to the top of an 8,600 foot ridge. Here, it crosses an intermittent stream at 6.5 miles and forks. The right fork switchbacks up 485 feet in a half mile to Moose Creek Divide, the boundary line between Targhee National Forest and Grand Teton National Park. The Divide marks the official start of Teton Crest Trail, which drops into the park and heads north to Hurricane Pass.

The left fork leads 1.4 miles to Moose Lake, the largest of eight lakes at the head of Moose Canyon. For a description of the route, see the Tram to Moose Lake Hike.

▲

28 GAME CREEK & HOUSETOP MTN.

Distance:
  Game Creek Divide: 13.8 miles RT
  Housetop Mountain : 16 miles RT
Elevation gained:
  Game Creek Divid: 3,610 ft.
  Housetop Mountain: 4,147 ft.
Maximum elevation:
  Game Creek Divide: 10,000 ft.
  Housetop Mountain: 10,537 ft.
Maps:
  Rendezvous Peak
  Victor

Because there is no fishing up Game Creek Canyon, this lonely trail on the west side of the Tetons is used almost exclusively by hunters in the fall and the occasional hiker in the summer. Trail blazes and cairns help mark the often-sketchy path to the top of the divide, where one gets a beautiful look into the western side of the Teton Range. Those with the time and energy may consider scrambling up the southeast ridge of Housetop Mountain for superb views of the upper reaches of Granite Canyon and the southernmost peaks of the Tetons.

To reach the trailhead drive west out of Jackson on Wyoming Hwy. 22 over Teton Pass to the town of Victor,

Idaho. Turn right in Victor onto the old Teton Pass Road and drive to the bridge crossing of Game Creek. Continue south, turning left at the second road after the bridge, roughly two miles from Victor. Follow this road up the canyon for approximately one mile to the trailhead. This is marked by a Forest Service sign and there is a small irrigation dam spanning the creek here.

Park and cross the log bridge to the start of the trail on the creek's north side. The trail begins its gradual but steady ascent towards the Divide, climbing through scattered lodgepole pine and meadows. At two miles the North Fork of Game Creek flows into the main stream on your left, making it necessary to cross its outlet to continue up the trail. There is a faint trail leading up that fork, but it is not maintained, is hard to follow, and soon fizzles out in heavy brush.

Cross the North Fork outlet and continue walking east. The South Fork of Game Creek tumbles down to the main stream at 2.7 miles. This fork of the river is used extensively by sheepherders during the summer months; be forewarned that all water in the region should be treated. An unofficial trail created by the herders parallels the South Fork, turning sharply south after roughly one more mile to join the trail down Plummer Canyon to Nordwall Campground. This route offers a possible loop option for those seeking a shorter day hike.

To reach Game Creek Divide, walk past the South Fork and continue up the canyon. The trail through this section is faint from little usage, but adequate tree blazes and cairns exist to guide you to the Divide; watch carefully for them. The rocky south side of 9,034 foot Baldy Knoll rises above you to your left as you ascend the canyon. At 3.8 miles, you ford Game Creek to its south side. Cross an intermittent stream at 4.0 miles, then recross Game Creek and a second intermittent stream at 4.5 miles. About the time your hiking boots are starting to lose their "squish," the trail crosses Game Creek again at just over six miles. Here it starts climbing more steeply, ascending 300 feet up the rocky cirque at the head of the canyon to Game Creek Divide, 6.9 miles from the trailhead.

The best vantage point of the east side of the Teton Range is from the summit of 10,537 foot Housetop Mountain, reached by following the ridge to your left (N) to the top of that peak. This involves ascending another 537 feet in 1.1 miles to reach the summit.

From the top, Marion Lake lies directly below you. Granite Canyon and Mount Hunt stretch to the east; Spearhead Peak and Fossil Mountain rise to the northeast, while views into Fox Creek Canyon lie to the northwest. Coal Creek Canyon and Taylor Mountain encompass the southern vista — all making the non-technical scramble to the top of Housetop a worthwhile culmination of this trip.

From the Divide it is also possible to make a rugged, but rewarding east-west range traverse. The descent to the Marion Lake/North Fork trail is little used and difficult to follow, and some route-finding is necessary to complete this one-mile section.

29 DARBY WIND AND ICE CAVES

Distance:
 Wind Cave: 2.6 miles one-way
 Ice Cave: 3.2 miles one-way
Elevation gain:
 Wind Cave: 1,870 ft.
 Ice Cave: 2,410 ft.
Maximum elevation:
 Wind Cave: 8,940 ft.
 Ice Cave: 9,400 ft.
Maps:
 Mount Bannon

A pair of interesting caves up Darby Canyon is the major draw of this popular west slope hike, closely followed by the intermittent waterfalls splashing down the canyon rim and impressive wildflower displays at peak bloom.

The existence of the caves is well-known to Teton Valley, Idaho, residents. They made their first guidebook appearance over 35 years ago in Orrin and Lorraine Bonney's classic, out-of-print, "Guide to Wyoming Mountains and Wilderness Areas." The Wind Cave snakes through the Darby Formation, a thick layer of 350 million year-old dolomite that gives the canyon its name. It plunges and climbs up several 40-50 foot drops along its three-quarter mile course, making climbing equipment and headlamps a necessity for those who wish to explore it. Open at both ends, wind often whistles through the rock tunnel, hence its moniker.

Unlike the Wind Cave, the Ice Cave doesn't parallel the canyon wall but leads deeper underground. Cooler temperatures lend to the creation of ethereal ice stalactites and stalagmites that are a wonder to see. Unfortunately, vandals and unthinking visitors occasionally damage the cave's features by carving their initials in the ice and knocking down the fragile formations—damage that takes years to repair. Don't leave your mark.

To reach the trailhead to both caves, drive west out of Jackson over Teton Pass on Wyoming Hwy. 22. Stay on the highway (renamed Idaho 33 once you cross the state line), and set your odometer as you leave the town of Victor. Drive 5.5 miles north and turn right unto a paved road. A sign for Darby Girls Camp is near its entrance. Stay right where the road forks at 1.6 miles. Drive another six miles to its end and park.

The trail begins at the footbridge over Darby Creek. It gradually climbs east through trees for the first .5 miles,

Waterfalls pouring off the canyon wall are common in the upper reaches of Darby early in the season, particularly in front of the Wind Cave.

where it crosses the South Fork of Darby Creek and enters the signed Jedediah Smith Wilderness Area. Here, it begins a sustained, steeper climb up the canyon, gaining 1,160 feet in the next 1.3 miles. At 1.8 miles, the trail enters Darby's upper basin and turns sharply right (W), crossing the creek before entering the woods. This is your first chance to glimpse the entrance of the Wind Cave on the west side of the canyon wall ahead of you. Early in the summer and in wet seasons, a waterfall bounces from the cave's entrance down the rocky wall. At 2.2 miles the trail divides.

To reach the Wind Cave:

Stay right and cross the creek. In a short distance, you'll reach a rock and cement memorial, constructed in remembrance of five hikers from Darby Girls Camp who died near the spot after being struck by lightning. From the monument, steep switchbacks lead to the cave's entrance, reached in another .4 miles

To visit the Ice Cave:

Go left at the junction. The trail parallels the creek for .2 miles, where it reaches another junction. Stay right. (The faint, unmaintained trail to the left climbs SE for two miles to a saddle west of 10,916 foot Fossil Mountain at the head of the canyon. The abandoned trail—which often disappears—then drops steeply south for another mile to an intersection with the Fox Creek Trail.) The trail to the Ice Caves parallels the creek, eventually crossing it. The last .3 miles to the cave's entrance is a steep scramble up rocky slopes, often snow-covered late in the season.

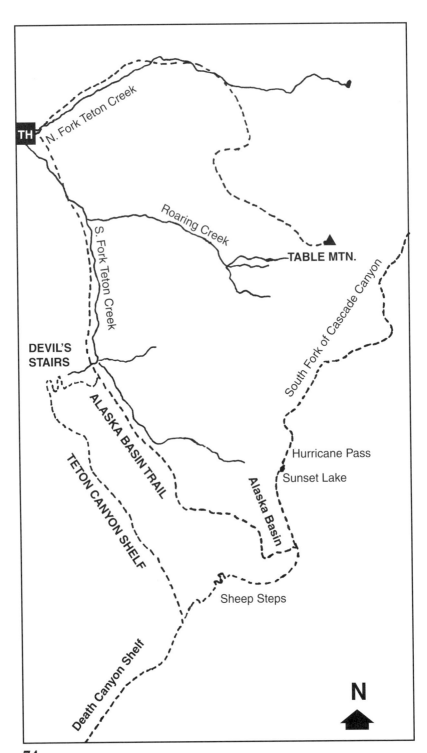

SOUTH TETON CANYON

▲

30 DEVIL'S STAIRS & TETON SHELF
31 ALASKA BASIN

Distance:
- Top of Devil's Stairs: 3.9 miles one-way
- End of Teton Canyon Shelf: 6.6 miles one-way
- Alaska Basin (Basin Lakes): 7 mile one-way

Elevation gained:
- Devil's Stairs: 1,565 ft.
- Teton Canyon Shelf: 2,745 ft.
- Basin Lakes: 2,605 ft.

Maximum elevation:
- Devil's Stairs: 8,520 ft.
- Teton Canyon Shelf: 9,700 ft.
- Basin Lakes: 9,560 ft.

Maps:
- Grand Teton
- Mount Bannon

Broad, gentle South Teton Canyon is the western slope's equivalent of Cascade Canyon: its beauty and accessibility draws more hikers than any other place on this side of the Tetons. A hike up steep Devil's Stairs leads to Teton Canyon Shelf, an interesting bench with good campsites and expansive views of Alaska Basin and 10,679 foot Battleship Mountain. Run-off streams and springs are plentiful on the bench, and the chance of seeing the mountain sheep that roam between Mounts Meek, Jedediah Smith and Bannon to the southwest is better than average. The series of vertical limestone caves and sink holes along the west side of the bench are also fun to explore.

Beyond the junction to Devil's Stairs the trail up South Teton Canyon climbs a series of glacial benches to reach the high alpine meadows of Alaska Basin and Basin Lakes. There, eight small ponds reflect the impressive cliffs of The Wall, a limestone formation that rings the surrounding area. Snow lingers in the basin until late in the season, giving the high region its name and providing a constant source of water for the fields of wildflowers that color this lovely spot. Bluebells, Indian paintbrush, columbine, forget-me-nots and astors all grow in wild profusion.

To reach the South Teton Canyon trailhead follow the instructions given for the Table Mountain Hike, No. 22. The well-signed trail begins as an old jeep track. It soon crosses the North Fork of Teton Creek and heads in a southeastern direction through a pleasant forest of fir and lodgepole pine. At .4 miles, you cross an intermittent stream. A close look at the short rock walls on your left may reveal rock climbers practicing their moves on the small cliffs.

At roughly three-quarters mile you'll cross a bridge over the South Fork of Teton Creek. Another quarter-mile up the trail, Roaring Creek cascades down the cliffs on your left (E). The trail stays right of South Teton Creek as it courses in-and-out of forest and meadows the next 1.8 miles to its junction with Devil's Stairs and the Teton Canyon Shelf Trail at 2.8 miles. The trail to the junction is quite flat, gaining only 445 feet in close to three miles.

Devil's Stairs and Teton Canyon Shelf

It doesn't take much imagination to see why the trail leading to your right is named "Devil's Stairs." The trail switchbacks its way up to a notch created by a stream spilling off the limestone cliffs of Teton Canyon Shelf above you. It is so steep that horses cannot navigate the route. Backpackers may wish they hadn't tried! Proceed straight up to the toe of the cliff band for roughly half a mile before switchbacking four times to gain the lower end of Teton Canyon Shelf at 8,520 feet, a gain of over one thousand feet in only 1.1 miles.

Once on the shelf, you soon cross the stream that created the notch. This provides a nice place to rest, refill your water bottles, and enjoy the view of the canyon below you. Alaska Basin lies to the east. Distinctive Battleship Mountain rises to the northeast and Buck Mountain rears up roughly 2.5 miles to the southeast. Ahead of you the canyon shelf, ranging from a quarter to a half mile wide, extends for over two miles to its end near 9,726 foot Mount Meek Pass. At 6.6 miles the trail along the shelf intersects the Teton Crest Trail.

The shelf is a great place to camp, enjoy the views, look for mountain sheep, and explore the caves in the limestone cliffs to your west. These cliffs range in elevation between 10,000 and 10,600 feet, the high point being 10,681 foot Mount Meek at the shelf's southwestern end. The shelf receives far less traffic than the more popular Alaska Basin below it, but in many ways is just as spectacular.

Alaska Basin

For hikers and/or backpackers wishing to reach Alaska Basin, walk past the junction to Devil's Stairs and continue on the main trail. This soon steepens as it works its way up a series of glacial benches, hitting the first a half-mile beyond the junction. A mile beyond the junction, you'll cross South Teton Creek and climb four switchbacks to a second bench that offers good camping.

Leaving the flatter bench, the trail climbs several switchbacks before re-

The hike up Devil's Stairs and Teton Canyon Shelf is memorable for its steepness and stunning scenery.

crossing South Teton Creek at roughly five miles. It crosses the outflow of Sunset Lake at 5.6 miles as you enter Alaska Basin at the head of the canyon. The trail gains a final glacial bench in the next 1.4 miles, rising from 8,800 feet to just under 9,600 feet on its way to Basin Lakes. A quarter mile before the lakes the trail through the Basin intersects Teton Crest Trail. A right turn takes you to the first of eight small lakes clustered on the high alpine floor.

From the junction with the Crest trail, it is 2.6 miles to 10, 600 foot Hurricane Pass to the north, and 2.4 miles to 9,726 foot **Mount Meek Pass** to the southwest. The trail from Basin Lakes over **Hurricane Pass** leads down the South Fork of Cascade Canyon to the valley floor on the east side of the Teton Range, a 14.2 mile hike.

The trail from the top of Mount Meek Pass, over **Death Canyon Shelf** and down Fox Creek Canyon brings you back to the valley floor on the west side of the range, a total of 12.8 miles.

32 TABLE MOUNTAIN

Distance:
 12.4 miles RT
Elevation gain:
 4,151 ft.
Maximum elevation:
 11,106 ft.
Maps:
 Granite Basin
 Mount Moran
 Grand Teton

From the flat-topped summit of Table Mountain (11,106 feet), pioneer photographer William Jackson of the famed Hayden Expedition took the first photographs of the Grand Teton in 1872. These spectacular pictures ultimately led to the range being designated public land, protected first by the Forest Service and later the National Park Service. There is no better vantage point in the Tetons for close-up views of the massive west face of the Grand, upper reaches of Cascade Canyon, or the U-shaped glacial valleys and canyons on the west side of the Tetons. This hike is widely regarded as one of the most outstanding in the entire region.

The trail starts from the parking area in Teton Canyon. Drive 33 miles from Jackson to Driggs via Teton Pass on Wyoming Hwy. 22 (the route changes to Idaho 33 when you cross the state line). Turn right in the center of Driggs, Idaho at the sign directing you to Alta, Wyoming, and Grand Targhee Ski Area. Drive through Alta to the Teton Canyon/Treasure Mountain Camp sign on the right-hand side of the road. Turn onto this road and continue another five miles to its end. The trail to Table Mountain follows the North Fork of Teton Creek. It's start is marked by a trailhead sign adjacent to the parking lot.

The first half-mile of the trail climbs steadily through aspens, paralleling but out-of-sight of the North Fork. As the grade levels out it traverses meadows filled with wildflowers and patches of forest.

At 1.4 miles, you'll pass the intersection to South Leigh Creek and Fred's Mountain to the left. Bear right to Table Mountain, heading up the wide valley. A snowy, knife-edge headwall is visible well ahead of you. The trail alternately climbs and levels out, wandering through lush flower-laden meadows and ascending rocky slabs.

It crosses the creek three times before reaching the base of the cirque below Table Mountain, clearly visible to the southeast. This basin consistently has one of the most spectacular

The Grand Teton, as seen from the summit of Table Mountain.

wildflower displays in the range. Bluebells, lupine, paintbrush, columbine, cow parsnip and many other varieties grow in profusion.

At four miles the trail makes its final creek crossing and winds steeply up the side of the cirque. Snow may hug the north-facing slopes of the cirque's headwall well into July. For this reason, Table Mountain is not a good early season choice unless you bring an ice axe and know how to travel safely on snow.

The top of the headwall accesses the west end of a long, high plateau 1,000 feet below and a mile away from Table's 11,106 ft. crown. From here, stunning views of Alaska basin and Teton Canyon unfold to the south. Looking down into the cirque you just exited may reveal moose or deer.

From the plateau it is an easy walk up gentle talus slopes to the summit block. The trail fades out about a half mile before the top but the route is obvious. To gain the summit, follow the steep, well-worn path. Proceed carefully, as the rubble is quite loose.

Don't be surprised if you see pack animals on the trail. Since Jackson and his mule, Molly, carried heavy photographic plates up the mountain, horses have been a popular mode of transport for people as well.

33 GREEN LAKES/SOUTH LEIGH

Distance:
    10.6 miles RT
Elevation gain:
    2,200 ft.
Maximum elevation:
    9,245 ft.
Maps:
    Granite Basin

A relatively easy hike to a cluster of pretty lakes on the west side of the Tetons makes Green Lakes a frequent goal for hikers living on both sides of the range. Native cutthroat trout populate the upper three lakes, drawing area fishermen as well.

To reach the trailhead, drive west out of Jackson over Teton Pass on Wyoming Highway 22. Stay on the highway (renamed Idaho 33 once you cross the state line) for 5.5 miles past the town of Driggs, where the road curves sharply to the left. Leave the highway here, taking the northbound turnoff dead ahead. Turn at the first right and proceed a little under three miles to a sign that directs you left to the North Leigh Creek Trail. Drive approximately four more miles, following a jeep track past the Dry Ridge trail sign to the Green Mountain/Tin Cup trail sign a short distance ahead. Park near the end of the track.

The signed trail immediately crosses Tin Cup Creek then switchbacks above it to a low, wooded ridge. Once on top it follows an old roadbed a short distance before dividing at 1.5 miles. The right fork heads south along the Andy Stone Trail. Take the left fork. The trail soon ascends a series of steep switchbacks. At the top of these it crosses a long, open slope that explodes with lush wildflowers in early summer. You'll enjoy the green-and-gold patchwork of Idaho farmland and distant blue Lehmi Mountains on the western horizon as you walk up the slope to the low end of a ridge, roughly three miles from the trailhead. Here, the trail turns right and ascends the ridgeline for another three-quarters of a mile to its high point of 9,245 feet, providing fine views of North Leigh Canyon below.

Dropping quickly off the ridge down a steep couloir, it turns right at the base of Green Mountain and climbs a small knoll before forking at five miles. Turn left to reach Green Lake, the largest lake in a cluster of four. The trail to the right traverses above Green, circles the smaller lakes and turns south, reaching Granite Basin 6.7 miles from the trailhead.

Many and varied wildflowers are a bonus on the hike to Green Lakes in mid-summer. One of the variety that thrives is monkshood, colored a rich, velvety purple.

Green Lake is bordered on the south and west by 9,614 foot Green Mountain. Double-summit Cleaver Peak and Maidenform Peak lie to the east, Window Peak is to the northeast.

Hikers desiring a longer walk can do a 12.8 mile loop by walking to Granite Basin and following the South Fork of North Leigh Creek back to the parking area (identified as the Andy Stone Trail on the topo map). If you select this pleasant option be sure to bring the Granite Basin quad and a compass, as there are numerous poorly signed trails in the region. It would be relatively easy to hike down the wrong one, necessitating an unplanned hitchhike back to your vehicle at the end of the day.

TETON PASS
▲

The history of Jackson Hole is largely a history of traffic over Teton Pass at the west edge of the valley. For Indians and trappers it was the trading route to Pierre's Hole in Idaho. For the first permanent settlers, the 8,431 foot divide was the sole year-round link to the outside world. Access to mail, groceries, clothing, hardware supplies and other equipment depended on this route to the nearest railhead in St. Anthony, Idaho, staying open.

The first known white men to cross the natural divide were members of the 1811 Astoria party. Led by Wilson Price Hunt, the group of 60 explorers and trappers under the employ of the Pacific Fur Company crossed the pass into Idaho while searching for an overland route to the Pacific. The famous mountain man Rendezvous of 1832 brought literally hundreds of men and thousands of animals over the same route. But when the fur trade died out, so did traffic over the pass.

It was not until Mormon families and other settlers from Idaho regularly crossed the divide to homestead in the valley that the need for a road was recognized. Uinta County, then the governmental seat for most of Jackson Hole, appropriated $500 for the project and hired Otho E. Williams to survey a route. Lacking proper equipment, Williams used a walnut table leaf as a surveying tool. The resulting passage had grades as high as 19°, and was so steep that heavy wagons routinely dragged trees behind them to keep them from running over their horse teams.

A half-dozen years after the road was built the Oregon Short Line Railroad put in a line between St. Anthony and Victor, Idaho, and daily stages subsequently began running mail and passengers between Victor and Wilson. In the summer the transport was a wagon and later a truck; in the winter months it consisted of a horse team and sleighs.

For years automobile traffic was limited to the brief summer season, as the pass was not regularly plowed. After keeping the pass open for two winters the State Highway Department announced in January of 1940 that clearing snow off the steep road was too costly, and stopped plowing it. Residents took matters into their own hands by confiscating the equipment and clearing the 5.5 mile road themselves. That modern-day vigilante story made national news. When tempers cooled, the keys were returned and the threatened lawsuit was dropped. Since then the highway department has never again said they would not plow this road.

Teton Pass marks the divide between the Teton Range to the north and the Snake River Range to the south. It is situated below 10,086 foot Mount Glory, a peak whose notorious east-facing Glory Bowl frequently avalanches in winter, occasionally closing the road for days at a time.

In addition to its winter attraction to backcountry skiers, the pass draws summer recreationists, offering a variety of trails with superb views of Jackson Hole as well as access to the west slope of the Tetons and the Snake River Range. Some of the favorites include trails to Ski Lake, Phillips Pass, the Ridgetop Trail and the trail down Black Canyon on the northernmost boundary of the Snake River Range. All are administered by the Jackson Ranger District of Bridger-Teton National Forest. For further information, contact the office by writing to:

>Jackson Ranger District
>Box 1689
>Jackson, Wyoming 83001
>307-739-5400

The western side is administered by the Teton Basin Ranger District of Targhee National Forest. For further information contact:

>Teton Basin Ranger District
>Driggs, Idaho 83422
>208-354-2431

34 RIDGETOP TRAIL
35 BLACK CANYON
36 OLD PASS ROAD

Distance:
  Ridgetop Trail: 4 miles RT
  Black Canyon: 6 miles one-way
  Old Pass Road: 4 miles one-way
Elevation Change:
  Ridgetop Trail: 848 ft.
  Black Canyon
    Gain: 849 ft.
    Loss: 2,685 ft.
  Old Pass Road: 1,916 ft.
Maximum Elevation:
  Ridgetop Trail: 9,279 ft.
  Black Canyon: 9,200 ft.
  Old Pass Road: 8,431 ft.

Several hiking trails start at the top of 8,431 foot Teton Pass, giving the hiker the option of staying high, descending, or dropping down and then climbing back to the top in a loop hike. Framed by the Gros Ventre Range, the southern end of Jackson Hole lies 2,200 feet below you. Wilson, the silver-corded Snake River, Snow King Mountain and East and West Gros Ventre Buttes are clearly seen from the parking area which is the starting point for the three options suggested here.

To reach the top of the Pass, turn right onto Wyoming Hwy. 22 from south Jackson and drive seven miles to the town of Wilson at the base of the pass. The road rises 2,224 feet in its 5.5 mile climb to the parking area on top.

Ridgetop Trail

As its name implies, the Ridgetop Trail follows a high crest of the Snake River Range and offers good views of these mountains and the valley floor to the east. The trail begins at the east end of the parking area and heads due south, climbing just over 200 feet in the first quarter-mile to a communications tower at 8,637 feet. A service road at the west end of the parking area also leads to the tower.

From there it continues its southerly direction along the east side of

85

the ridge. At the one mile mark it skirts the upper end of big, open slopes and goes into the trees. The trail alternately passes through trees and small meadows before reaching a broad clearing overlooking the head of Black Canyon and the rest of the range spread out to the south. Here, it crosses to a clearing west of Peak 9,279 on your left. An old sign high on a tree directs you left to Black Canyon. This is the turn-around point for the Ridgetop Trail.

Black Canyon

From the trailhead sign the path down heavily-forested Black Canyon drops 1,000 feet the first mile, descending south for .3 miles to a wooded saddle before heading due east down the drainage. A half mile below the saddle the open southeast slopes of Peak 9,279 rise above you to the left. On the right side of the trail Black Canyon Creek begins, closely following the path to the mouth of the canyon. The open slopes soon disappear as the trail re-enters the forest and descends the canyon at a moderate grade. The canyon narrows considerably below this, broadening out somewhat in its last 1.5 miles to meet an old jeep road at its mouth. There, the trail/road swings sharply north, reaching the barrier at the base of the Old Pass Road in a half-mile, a total of six miles from the top of the pass. Shuttle a car in advance if you don't want to catch a ride back up. Or, plan on hiking up the Old Pass Road back to your car, a 10 mile loop hike.

Old Pass Road

Only four miles from the top of the Pass to the plowed berm just beyond Trail Creek Ranch, the Old Pass Road was the main highway until the present pass was completed in 1970. Switchbacking eight times — five in the short section bordering the western side of Glory Slide — the former road had grades close to 15 percent and was subject to dangerous avalanche activity that claimed the life of more than one resident. Although the present pass is still prone to avalanche, it is much less exposed to this winter hazard and the grade is much more moderate.

The abandoned roadway is heavily used by skiers in the winter and hikers and mountain bikers in the summer. Starting a short distance due east from the top of the pass, it gradually descends for three-quarters of a mile before switchbacking steeply down 2.8 miles to tiny Crater Lake. Nestled by a sharp curve at 7,160 feet, the deep blue lake lies at the toe of Glory Slide in a natural depression, formed from repeated slides melting at the same spot.

The descent from the lake to the end of the old road is moderate. Hikers enjoy great views of the Gros Ventres in front of them as they lose elevation, and are treated to a profusion of wildflowers in mid-summer. The flowers thrive alongside the road, aided by run-off funneled down the slight slope of the roadbed. The hike up the road to Crater Lake is a very popular short walk, as well.

Those wanting to shuttle a car or hike up the old road can access its start by driving one mile up the pass and turning left onto the road across from the Heidelberg Inn. Park one mile further in, near the plowed earth barrier at the end of the driveable road.

37 SKI LAKE

Distance:
  3 miles RT
Elevation gained:
  760 ft
Maximum elevation:
  8,720 ft.
Maps:
  Rendezvous Peak

Ski Lake is an early-season favorite, as well as a classic place to enjoy wildflowers in mid-summer. The short, well-traveled trail starts halfway up Teton Pass, allowing hikers who have yet to acquire their summer legs and lungs the luxury of climbing under 1,000 feet — but still being rewarded with telescopic vistas of the distant Snake River and Gros Ventre ranges on the way to the lake. Nestled snuggly in a cirque at the southern end of the Teton Range, Ski Lake's dark blue water is virtually hidden until the very last moment.

From the town of Wilson, drive up Teton Pass on Wyoming Hwy. 22 to the marked Phillips Canyon Road on your right. The steep, rocky dirt road soon becomes a jeep trail that peters out after several miles. Rough conditions mean you can rarely drive more than another half-mile: it is best to simply park near the turn-off.

Walk up the road until you see a signed, obvious trail heading through the sage-covered slopes on your left. The trail winds along the hillside and crosses a prominent draw before it comes to an unmarked junction at the edge of a meadow at a half mile. The trail to the lake turns left and skirts the boggy south end of the meadow, crossing a tributary drainage and winding northwest into scattered trees before crossing an intermittent creek at the one mile mark. Pass an old campsite and re-enter groves of trees before crossing the outflow of Ski Lake Creek at 1.4 miles.

The lake is reached .1 miles further. It's south shore is bordered by thick conifers, the west side by a talus slope spilling down from an unnamed 9,500 foot knob above it. While the hike itself is short, allow plenty of time to relax and enjoy the lake—and the vast array of wildflowers so abundant that naturalists choose it for wildflower walks. It is attractive for the same reason to photographers.

Hikers wishing to extend their day often follow an unmarked trail north and west of the lake, ascending a 9,734 foot ridge roughly one mile further. From here it is possible to proceed west into Coal and Mesquite Creeks, or stay on top of the ridge until it circles the Middle Fork Amphitheater and drops east towards Phillips Pass.

38 MAIL CABIN CANYON

Distance:
    4 miles one-way
Elevation gain:
    2,100 ft.
Maximum elevation:
    9,100 ft.
Maps:
    Rendezvous Peak
    Teton Pass
    Palisades Peak
    Victor

Hikers looking for an alternative to the Old Pass Road should consider the trail up Mail Cabin Canyon. Four miles of uphill hiking brings you to the head of the canyon, which marks the divide between the Teton River drainage to the west and Snake River drainage to the east. From there, you can hike down Mosquito Creek or the North Fork of the Palisades, or return to Teton Valley Idaho via Mikesell Canyon or Burbank Creek.

The trail starts at a signed turn-off on the west side of Teton Pass. Drive seven miles west of Jackson on Wyoming Hwy. 22 to the town of Wilson. Set your odometer when you pass Hungry Jack's General Store. From there it is 5.5 miles up the winding pass road to the top of the pass, marked by a large parking area/scenic turnout to your left. Descend 2.6 miles to the signed Mail Cabin Creek turnout, a total of 8.1 miles from Hungry Jack's. Pull into the entrance and park off the road

The dirt road up the canyon immediately crosses a tributary of Trail Creek and proceeds south on a level course for .6 miles to a second unbridged creek crossing. A third follows .1 mile further. Beyond the last crossing, the wide dirt track narrows to trail width and begins a steady climb above Mail Cabin Creek through pleasant pine forest.

The narrow canyon widens at 2.5 miles. Here the creek courses through a pretty meadow. A half-mile further, the trail turns right (W) away from the stream and climbs steeply up a wooded hillside—gaining over 400 feet in .2 miles—then turns north and angles up an open slope covered with wildflowers in mid-summer. At the end of the traverse, the trail reaches a small saddle, marked by elevation 8,620 on the Palisades Peak topo Map. Here, the Mail Cabin Trail turns left (S), and contours through wooded

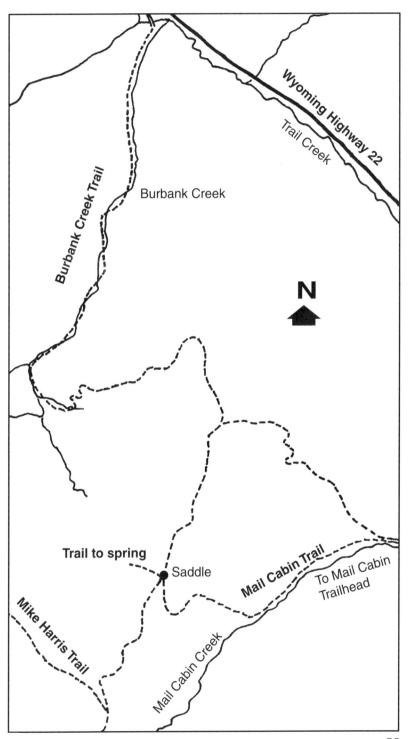

before intersecting the Mike Harris Trail at the head of the canyon. That pack trail heads right (NW) to Mikesell Canyon, south to Mosquito Pass and the North Fork of the Palisades trail. The view of the Palisades just beyond the trail junction is spectacular.

By walking due west from saddle 8,620, you quickly pick up a horse trail that steeply drops to a spring and dead-ends. To hike down Burbank Creek, walk sharply right (N) from the saddle, ascending towards treeline. Once inside the forest, you'll soon gain a clear trail that climbs for 200 feet before reaching a ridge. This trail reaches Wyoming Hwy. 22 via Burbank Creek in 4.1 miles. See hike no. 39. From the Burbank Creek trailhead, it is 2.8 miles to the Mail Cabin Creek turnoff. Assuming you park at least .1 miles inside the entrance, the loop hike is 10.5 miles if you don't do a car shuttle between the two trailheads.

▲

---

39 BURBANK CREEK

Distance:
    4.1 miles one-way
Elevation gain:
    2,020 ft.
Maximum elevation:
    8,020 ft.
Maps:
    Victor
    Palisades Peak

Halfway up Burbank Creek last summer, my hiking companion turned around and pointedly asked, "Are there trails you decide *not* to put in a book?"

I understood his thinly-veiled exasperation. We had been slogging in-and-out of Burbank Creek on a muddy, sloppy trail for over an hour. The topo map shows 11 crossings; the official count from the district Forest Service office is 25. The truth probably lies between the two. I had lost count.

To answer the question, yes, there are many trails and routes I don't put in books. I decided to include this mess of a trail for a number of reasons. First, it's a great place to walk your dog on a hot summer day. Finding water is not a problem, and canine critters love splashing in the creek. Second, it's a wonderful place for gathering berries in the fall, particularly the under-rated gooseberry. Last, the upper dry sections of the hike cuts through impressive old forest before opening up to sweeping, high country views. It's worth the muck.

To reach the trailhead, drive seven miles west of Jackson on Wyoming Hwy. 22 to the town of Wilson. Set your odometer as you pass Hungry Jack's General Store on your right. It is 5.5 miles to the top of Teton Pass, marked by a large parking area/scenic turnout on your left. The road drops steeply west, reaching the signed Burbank Creek turn-off to your left 10.8 miles from Hungry Jack's (5.3 miles from the top of the pass). Pull in and park.

Cross a footbridge over Trail Creek and begin walking south. The trail hopscotches endlessly over Burbank Creek before turning left (SE) and climbing through trees to drier ground at the two mile mark.

At three miles, it turns left (S) again and climbs to an open ridge that provides good views of the surrounding terrain. Although the 1978 Victor topo shows a trail to Mail Cabin Creek heading east at 3.5 miles, one isn't apparent on the ground. Continue ascending south to reach the high point of the trail at 3.8 miles and 8,820 feet. Here, the trail drops 200 feet to a small saddle, identified by elevation 8,620 on the Palisades Peak topo. Loop back to Wyoming Hwy. 22 via Mail Cabin Creek— see hike no. 38— or retrace your steps.

Those with time and energy will be well-rewarded by hiking the additional .5 miles to the upper end of the Mail Cabin Canyon Trail. The scene at this trail intersection is quite spectacular.

The view near the intersection of the Burbank/Mail Cabin Canyon trails.

40 OLIVER PEAK

Distance:
    4 miles one-way
Elevation gain:
    2,324 ft.
Maximum elevation:
    9,004 ft.
Maps:
    Victor

An easy scramble up Oliver Peak, accessed off a well-maintained trail, yields nice views of the southern end of the Tetons and the lightly-visited Snake River Range. This appealing hike draws far fewer people than trails in Grand Teton National Park, and because it travels through land administered by the Forest Service, you can take your dog.

The trailhead is located off the west side of Teton Pass. Drive south of downtown Jackson on U.S. Hwy. 89/191 to the junction with Wyoming Hwy. 22. Turn right and drive seven miles to Wilson, located at the base of the pass. The road gains over 2,200 feet in the next 5.5 miles, cresting at an elevation of 8,431 feet. From the top of the pass, drop west 8.2 miles to the well-signed entrance to Mike Harris Campground on the left side of the road. Turn into the campground, cross the bridge, and immediately turn left unto a rough dirt road signed "Mike Harris Trail." Go as far as you want to punish your car and park. In .5 miles, the rough road divides at a wooden Forest Service Post missing its signage. Walk up the right branch of the road: It soon narrows to a trail.

The trail gently ascends a shady draw sprinkled with bluebells, columbine, clematis and delicate wood violets. It turns sharply right (N) at .4 miles, then left .2 miles further. Here it starts steadily climbing up steeper terrain through stands of mature aspen and open meadows. The latter are dressed in snowy gentian, stickseed forget-me-not and fragrant Utah Honeysuckle bushes. Turn around occasionally for views of the southern end of the Tetons. As you approach the top of the ridge—marked by lichen-covered rocks and shimmering gold arnica in mid-summer—you've gained enough elevation to see the Grand Teton.

The crest of the ridge is reached at the two mile mark. Here, the trail bears left (SE) on an almost level

The high country surrounding Teton Pass is nicely viewed on the hike up Oliver Peak, accessed from the Mike Harris Trail on the west side.

course through pine and fir before ascending at a moderate grade to a grassy, open slope. Twenty-five yards ahead, the trail splits at 2.6 miles near a clump of trees. A poorly placed (and easily missed!) Forest Service sign directs you right to reach the head of Pole Canyon in four miles, Palisades Forks in five and Palisade Lake in nine.

To reach Oliver Peak, stay left at the junction. The trail climbs a grassy rise then gently contours down. Oliver Peak rises in front of you. Soon, the trail enters the trees and turns south towards open terrain at 3.6 miles. Leave the trail here, walking left (E) up the slopes of Oliver for .4 miles to reach the 9,004 foot summit, marked by a rock cairn. Here, the snowy peaks of the Palisades, the Snake River Range and the southern end of the Tetons circle the skyline.

Mike Harris Campground was named for an early resident who raised sheep and operated a sawmill where the campground is now located. Oliver Peak derives its moniker from the man who surveyed the area near the turn of the century.

▲

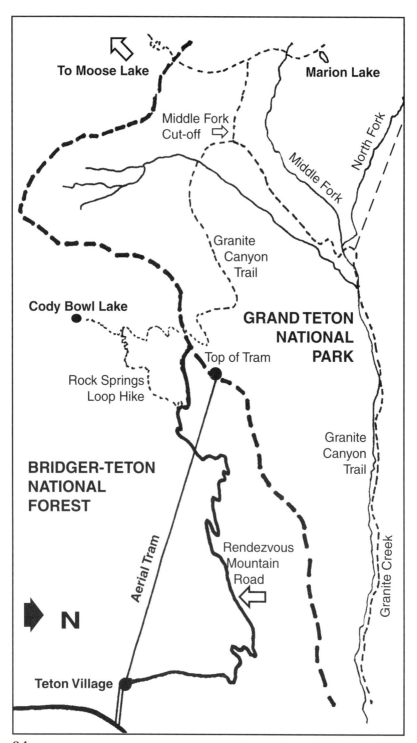

TETON VILLAGE

▲

On July 31, 1991, the aerial tram at Teton Village had its 25th birthday. Like all good parties there were balloons, prizes, music and lots of people on hand to celebrate its anniversary. Today the tram and eight lifts transport skiers from all over the world up the slopes of this famed resort. Covering over 3,000 acres, the ski area encompasses 10,450 foot Rendezvous Peak and one-and-a-half miles to the northeast, 8,426 foot Apres Vous Peak. Casper Bowl lies between the two.

The Village was only a twinkle in entrepreneur Paul McCollister's eye in 1961 when he and son Mike climbed to the top of Rendezvous Peak to look at surrounding slopes as a site for a potential ski area. The vast, open area excited him: he knew the length of the runs would be unparalleled anywhere in the United States. His enthusiasm attracted other investors, and following a ski tour the spring of 1963, the decision was made to proceed — a decision that propelled Jackson from a summer tourist town to a year-round destination resort.

Construction of the tram was begun the next year after dynamite and a snowcat cleared enough snow away from the base of the mountain to have a ground-breaking ceremony. The $2 million dollar, double-reversible tram system took over two years to complete, making its first passenger run on July 31, 1966.

Although conceived as a winter sports playground, the Village has turned into a popular summer resort as well. The 7.2 mile service road criss-crossing the Apres Vous and Rendezvous peaks makes an ideal trail down (or up!) from the top. A trail constructed by the National Park Service down the backside of Rendezvous after the ski area opened provides a connecting link to the Crest Trail, Granite Canyon, and destinations such as Moose Lake on the west slope of the Tetons. The Ski Corporation has also constructed several fine self-guided intrepretative trails, including the .3 mile Summit Loop Hike, the three mile Cody Bowl Hike, and the 4.2 mile Rock Springs Bowl Hike. Summer naturalists stationed on top of the mountain lead free interpretative walks.

The top of Rendezvous Mountain is one of the best places in the valley to view the meandering, braided path of the Snake River, dubbed "Mad River" by trappers who found the waterway difficult to float. The 666-mile waterway courses through Jackson Hole on its way to the Columbia River and eventually the Pacific Ocean. From the summit one can see Housetop Mountain, Battleship Mountain, Mount Meek and Fossil Peak, all rising on the crest between the Teton's east and west slopes.

Because of its high elevation, trails that start or lead to the top of the mountain are often closed due to snow until early July, if not later. For current information on mountain conditions, the cost of the aerial tram and operating hours, or to reserve a spot on a free naturalist hike, call the ski resort at 307-733-2292.

41 RENDEZVOUS PEAK

Distance:
   Teton Village to the Summit: 7.2 miles
Elevation gain:
   4,139 ft.
Maximum Elevation:
   10,450 ft.
Maps:
   Rendezvous Peak
   Teton Village

A 300 mile panoramic scene of seven mountain ranges, the Snake River, and "right there" views of Buck Mountain and the Grand Teton lure hikers to the summit of Peak 10,450. Peak 10,450? Yep, Peak 10,450. Following the construction of the Jackson Hole Ski Area the name Rendezvous has been frequently and mistakenly used for the peak. The real "Rendezvous" is 10,297 foot Rendezvous Mountain, a massive hunk of dirt and rock 2.7 miles to the southeast. Peak 10,450 is actually a subsummit on the eastern ridge of that complex massif.

Since Peak 10,450 unquestionably lacks a certain ring—and would confuse those used to the wrong nomenclature—it will be called Rendezvous in this description. It's summit can be reached by hiking up the ski area's dirt service road, built when the tram was being installed and the area first developed. The meandering 7.2 mile course rises over 4,100 feet on its way to the top. Most hikers prefer to ride the aerial tram up and walk down, but a large number also opt for the more aerobic choice of hiking up the route.

Drive south out of Jackson on U.S. Hwy 89/191, turning right onto Wyoming Hwy. 22 at the traffic light by McDonalds. Head west five miles to a bridge over the Snake River. Just over the bridge turn right onto Wyoming Hwy. 390 and drive seven miles to Teton Village, the resort complex at the base of the Jackson Hole Ski Area. The turnoff to the Village to the west is well-marked by a large wooden sign that identifies the ski area.

From the parking lot walk up the gentle slope on the right side of the clock tower. Veer right before you reach the Festival Hall in front of you. You'll see a low angle ski run about 60 yards ahead. The service road beings on the left side of the run.

The road heads north up Apres Vous Mountain before turning southwest and traversing across the lower slopes. Signs on the mountain direct you to the tram on top. You'll pass Casper Bowl, the Gros Ventres, and Thunder chair before reaching the bottom of Rendezvous Bowl. Steep switchbacks from the bottom of the bowl bring you

Cody Bowl, viewed from the hike up the service road at Teton Village.

to the top of the mountain. As you gasp your way up chew on this: Every fall, athletes competing in the Rendezvous Peak Run RUN up this stretch. The course record, bottom to top, is just under one hour.

Since the route is the service road the grade is more or less constant — a little steeper in some places and not quite so steep in others. The road winds in and out of the trees but is primarily in the open. Be sure to bring sufficient water for the hike. There is some run-off on the mountain's face but this dries up as the summer progresses, and in any case, it must be treated for safety.

Once on top, wander to the small rise behind the tram dock to peer from the telescope. On the dock itself signs identify the surrounding mountain ranges and notable peaks. Bring warm clothing with you so you can linger and soak in the outstanding view. The 10,450 foot summit is often windy, and mountain storms can develop quite quickly: 80° and calm at the base of the Village may be only 50° and windy on top of Rendezvous. At a minimum, a wool hat, lightweight gloves and a wind jacket are recommended gear for this outing.

Restrooms and a snack bar are located on the summit. Hikers who walk to the top earn a free ride down the aerial tram. The double-reversible system was brought on-line in 1966 after 26 months of construction. Since then it has been in almost constant operation, transporting millions of skiers, climbers, hikers and sightseers up and down the mountain.

42 ROCK SPRINGS BOWL

Distance:
   4.2 miles RT
Elevation gain:
   Approx. 500 ft.
Maximum elevation:
   10,450 ft.
Maps:
   Teton Village

The Rock Springs Bowl interpretative hike at the Jackson Hole Ski Area is a 4.2 mile loop through varied, rugged alpine terrain. An inexpensive trail map available at the Village introduces you to the alpine ecosystem: Engelmann spruce, whitebark pine, subalpine firs, and snow buttercups; pink snow; glacial cirques; Teton geology; the fossils and Karst topography of Cody Bowl; and the small animals that den in this high region.

To reach the ski area follow directions given in the preceding write-up. Take the aerial tram to the top of the Rendezvous Peak. The interpretative trail and other hiking routes down the mountain are opened when enough snow has melted off the east face of Rendezvous to allow safe trail travel, usually by late June/early July. Naturally, this varies from year-to-year. For information on trail conditions, tram prices and operating hours, call the Jackson Hole Ski Corporation at 733-2292.

Cutting across meadows, talus slopes and occasional snow patches, the Rock Springs Bowl interpretative trail is approximately 40% downhill and 60% uphill — a challenge for those not used to exercising at high altitude. Ski area officials recommend that you allow yourself four hours to complete the loop, which begins by walking left (S) down the ridge trail from the tram towards the Granite Canyon trailhead. Stay on the service road/hiking trail as it leaves the ridgetop and swings left (NE), dropping into Rendezvous Bowl. The steep subalpine slope is buried under 10-12 feet of compacted snow during the winter months. In the summer, small alpine wildflowers and stunted, wind deformed trees called krumholz cling to the bowl's steep sides and help hold the unstable soil layer on the 35 degree angle slope.

The service road/trail switchbacks down the face of Rendezvous. At the end of the second switchback you'll see a clearly marked trail heading straight off the switchback and traveling south across Rendezvous Trail, a man-made ski run. Leave the service road here and follow the trail into Rock Springs Bowl, a beautiful area that encompasses most of the hike.

Here you'll see examples of subalpine fir, the forces of wind, and steep rock cliffs and glacial cirques remnants of the last ice age 40,000 to 15,000 years ago. From early to mid summer you'll probably also see "pink snow," created by the red jello-like coating that encases algae growing in the snowfields (Warning: Do not eat it! Pink snow can cause severe diarrhea and intestinal disorders).

As you begin the uphill walk on the far side of the bowl you may spy bright yellow snow buttercups and animal dens that house ubiquitous ground squirrels, pocket gophers, marmots and pikas. The last is an earless little ball of fur that squeaks out a warning if you get too close.

Near the top of the loop the trail enters Cody Bowl, a small cirque that rests above Rock Springs Bowl. This glacial hollow holds special interest for fossil lovers, as it contains abundant amounts of marine corals and brachiopods in the remains of a shallow sea that covered the area 350 million years ago. The bowl is also the site of an unusual geological feature called Karst topography. Slightly acidic rainwater has dissolved the soft limestone rock in this area, creating a system of underground passages and caverns. Cody Bowl Lake, formed by meltwater, drains completely underground by late summer.

The marked trail climbs out of Cody Bowl and rejoins the trail leading back to the aerial tram dock. Naturalists also lead free hikes on both trails throughout the course of the summer. Call the Ski Corporation for advance reservations and information.

Persons hiking on top of the mountain are advised that it can be as much as 20-30 degrees cooler than the valley floor, and that the weather can change rapidly.

The aerial tram at Teton Village whisks people up the mountain.

43 MARION LAKE

Distance:
 12.4 miles RT
Elevation gain:
 1,600 ft. gain one-way
 2,810 ft. loss one-way
Maximum elevation:
 10,450 ft.
Maps:
 Teton Village
 Rendezvous Peak

Tucked at the base of rocky 10,537 foot Housetop Mountain, Marion Lake is one of the more popular day and overnight destinations in the southern end of the Teton Range. The up-and-down hike to the lake crosses the South, Middle and North Forks of Granite Creek before climbing a final bench to the small, aquamarine jewel. Moose and deer are often seen browsing in the high meadows and wildflowers abound. Good views of the backside of Rendezvous Peak and Granite Canyon add to this hike's appeal.

Drive south out of Jackson on U.S. Hwy 89/191, turning right onto Wyoming Hwy. 22 at the traffic light by McDonalds. Head west five miles to a bridge over the Snake River. Just over the bridge turn right onto Wyoming Hwy. 390 and drive seven miles to Teton Village, the resort complex at the base of the Jackson Hole Ski Area. The turnoff to the Village to the west is well-marked by a large wooden sign that identifies the ski area.

Take the aerial tram to the top of Rendezvous Peak. From the tram deck, walk left (S) down a windswept ridge towards Cody Peak. The ridge dips at the saddle between Rendezvous Peak and Peak 10,215 to the south. Here, you'll see a trail sign directing you to turn right to reach the Teton Village Parking Area, the Middle Fork Cutoff and Marion Lake. It is a little confusing, but this is the trail you want. It rapidly switchbacks down into a rocky cirque that often holds patches of snow late into the season. The numerous small streams trickling down from the snowfields above are flanked with scores of periwinkle bluebells and snowy white columbine. From the bottom of the cirque the trail climbs north to the top of a ridge on the opposite side, offering good views of the valley you just left and the backside of the tram station. It then drops again—angling south as it cuts across the bottom slope of Peak 10,215—and descends into the upper South Fork of Granite Canyon. At the head of the canyon the trail turns north, intersecting the Middle Fork Cutoff Trail at 3.5 miles.

Turn left and cross an intermittent stream at 3.7 miles. The trail crosses, then closely parallels, a second intermittent stream as it gradually gains 200 feet on its way to a junction with the Teton Crest Trail at 4.1 miles. Turn right here, dropping slightly as you walk towards the headwaters of the Middle Fork at 4.3 miles. Cross the narrow stream and begin the steep 600 foot climb to a 9,400 foot saddle west of the unnamed peak to your right. On top of the saddle, 5.2 miles from the trailhead, a little-used trail to your left leads to Game Creek Divide. If you have the time and energy it is worth the .6 mile side trip to the top of the Divide to look down the west side of the range.

From the saddle, the trail descends steeply to a junction with the North Fork Trail at 5.6 miles. This trail descends 8.2 miles down Granite Canyon to the valley floor. Stay left on the Crest Trail to reach the lake. Shortly cross the North Fork itself, and begin climbing steeply up the final slope before reaching the lake at 6.2 miles.

Resting at an elevation of 9,240 feet, the popular lake is named after Marion Danford, a guest at the Bar BC Dude Ranch in the valley in the early 1900s. From the lake it is possible to continue north to Fox Creek Pass and walk down either Fox Creek Canyon on the west slope of the Tetons, or Death Canyon on the east side. Those interested in returning via the tram should be sure to allow enough time to catch the last car of the day.

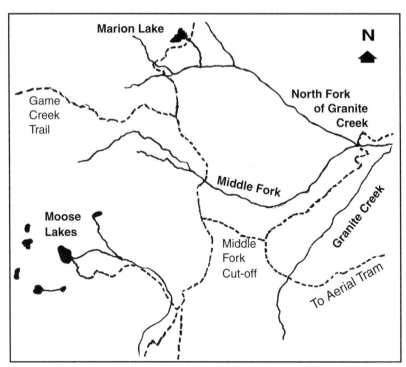

44 TRAM TO MOOSE LAKE

Distance:
  12.8 miles RT
Elevation loss:
  1,150 ft.
Maximum elevation:
  10,450 ft.
Maps:
  Teton Village
  Rendezvous Peak

Almost the same distance as Marion Lake and in many ways just as pretty, Moose Lake on the west slope of the Tetons draws far less traffic. The lake is the largest of eight ponds and lakes clustered on appealing limestone benches. The lakes are bordered to the west by a wall of 10,300 foot cliffs.

The outlet to Moose Lake is the headwater of Moose Creek, both named after the healthy population of Alces Americana that live in the basin and surrounding area. Unlike Marion Lake in Grand Teton National Park, I've rarely seen backpackers in this lovely spot. However, motorized trail bikes have ripped up the trail on more than one occasion, splitting the quiet and solitude of the area. Don't be surprised if you hear an engine: it is not your imagination.

Directions to the aerial tram at Teton Village are given in the hike up Rendezvous Peak, No. 41. From the tram deck, walk left (S) down a windswept ridge towards Cody Peak. The ridge dips at the saddle between Rendezvous Peak and Peak 10,215 to the south. Here, you'll see a trail sign directing you to turn right to reach the Teton Village Parking Area, the Middle Fork Cutoff and Marion Lake. The trail rapidly switchbacks down a rocky cirque that often holds patches of snow late into the season. Numerous small run-off streams from the snowfields above are flanked with scores of periwinkle bluebells and snowy white columbine.

At the bottom of the cirque, the trail climbs north to the top of a ridge on the opposite side, offering good views of the valley you just left and the backside of the tram station. It then drops again, angling south as it cuts across the bottom slope of Peak 10,215 and descends the upper south fork of Granite Canyon. At the head of the canyon the trail turns north, intersecting the Middle Fork Cutoff Trail at 3.5 miles.

Turn left here, walking slightly uphill through open slopes. The trail crosses two intermittent streams, usually dry by mid-August, before intersecting the Teton Crest Trail at 4.1 miles. Turn left unto that trail and begin the gentle ascent to 9,085 ft. Moose Creek Divide, the official start of the Crest Trail at Grand Teton National Park's southern boundary. You'll pass a small lake to your left just before you reach the top of the Divide. Horsepackers occasionally camp in the area, so if you draw water from the lake be sure to treat it. The Divide provides a nice view of the upper reaches of Moose Creek and Taylor Mountain to the southwest.

The trail descends four switchbacks to an intersection with the trail from Phillips Pass. Stay to your right and walk .1 miles to the intersection with Moose Creek Trail, 5.2 miles from the top of the aerial tram. Turn right unto the unsigned trail and soon cross Moose Creek. You'll recross the creek twice as you walk uphill to the lakes. A short but easy scramble up a 300 foot rock band brings you to the top of the first limestone bench and four of the eight lakes. Moose Lake (9,300 feet) is the largest. An east scramble up another 300 foot band at the south end of the lake provides access to the second limestone bench and four more lakes. From here, the view of Rendezvous Peak to the southeast is spectacular.

Like Death Canyon Shelf and Cody Bowl, much of the water on the limestone benches drains into underground passages.

▲

45 GRANITE CANYON

Distance:
 12.3 miles one-way
Elevation loss:
 4,100 ft.
Maximum elevation:
 10,450 ft.
Maps:
 Rendezvous Peak
 Teton Village

This is it: the only trail in the park that starts at the top of a mountain and winds its way down to the valley floor. From the summit of 10,450 foot Rendezvous Peak, the trail travels mostly downhill through a scenic canyon characterized by open meadows, scattered forest, rocky cliffs and frequent stretches of dense vegetation. It parallels pretty Granite Creek as it descends. Moose and deer frequent the canyon's lower stretches, an added bonus for wildlife lovers and photographers. It is not surprising that the newest trail in Grand Teton National Park is also one of the most popular.

To reach the aerial tram follow instructions given for the hike up Rendezvous Peak, No. 41. The double-reversal tram whisks you to the top of Rendezvous in eleven minutes, gaining 4,139 vertical feet as the cables pull you skyward. A panoramic sweep of mountains and the valley floor thousands of feet below greet you as you unboard — an enticing start for this 12.3 mile hike.

From the tram deck, walk left (S) down a windswept ridge towards Cody Peak. The ridge dips at the saddle between Rendezvous Peak and Peak 10,215 to the south. Here, you'll see a trail sign directing you to turn right to reach the Teton Village Parking Area, the Middle Fork Cutoff and Marion Lake. This is the one you want. It rapidly switchbacks down into a rocky cirque that often holds patches of snow late into the season. Numerous small run-off streams are flanked with scores of periwinkle bluebells and snowy white columbine.

From the bottom of the cirque the trail climbs north to the top of a ridge on the opposite side, offering good views of the valley you just left and the backside of the tram station. It then drops again—angling south as it cuts across the bottom slope of Peak 10,215—and descends the upper south fork of Granite Canyon.

At the head of the canyon the trail turns north, intersecting the Middle Fork Cutoff Trail at 3.5 miles.

Pass that junction and continue straight, descending the open ridge between the south and middle forks of the canyon. At the end of the ridge the trail switchbacks down to bridge crossings— first of Middle Fork Creek then North Fork Creek— to the upper Granite Canyon Patrol Cabin at 5.2 miles. At this intersection the Granite Canyon Trail goes left (W) to Marion Lake and right (E) to the base of Granite Canyon. Go right, following rushing Granite Creek as you continue down canyon. The trail is first close to, then above the stream as it winds in and out of forest and periodically crosses slopes covered with talus and avalanche debris swept down during the winter months.

Shortly after passing the lower Granite Canyon Patrol Cabin you'll come to the Valley Trail junction, 9.9 miles from the tram station. Turn right (W) to walk the 2.4 miles back to the Teton Village parking area. The last section of trail skirts the western base of Apres Vous Peak. Be forewarned that there is a lot of horse traffic in the area. If you see a horse party approaching, step off the trail to give the animals the right-of-way and to avoid spooking them.

A half-mile before reaching Teton Village you leave Grand Teton National Park and enter national forest land at the base of the ski area. A number of spur trails split off the main trail in this vicinity. All of them lead back to the parking area.

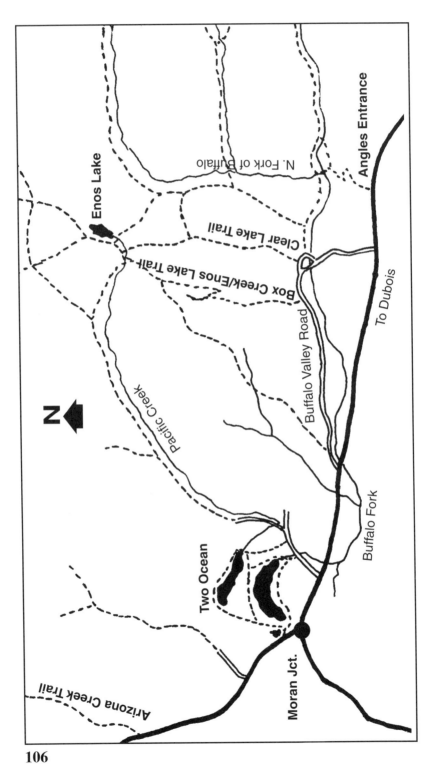

TETON WILDERNESS

▲

Close to 900 square miles in size, Teton Wilderness in Bridger-Teton National Forest abutts Washakie Wilderness to the east and Yellowstone National Park to the north. Its southern end borders the Gros Ventre Wilderness. To the west, it is rimmed by Grand Teton National Park. Three times bigger than the park itself, this immense expanse of meadows, forests, peaks and plateaus makes up the second largest wilderness area in the lower 48 states. Yet it's backcountry use is only a third of its famous neighbor. If you are seeking a wilderness experience, point your hiking boots towards this region.

The eastern end of the wilderness is characterized by the volcanic mountains and plateaus of the southern end of the Absaroka Range. The highest point in Teton Wilderness is 12,165 foot Younts Peak (the highest peak in the Absorka Range overall is 13,153 foot Francis Peak in the Washakie Wilderness). Breccia rock, a mixture of pebbles and stones loosely held together by lava, forms beautiful striated cliff bands that rise directly from flowered fields below. When the snow melts in the spring, intermittent waterfalls spill over the lips of the high volcanic plateaus in this huge pristine wilderness.

In contrast, the western half of Teton Wilderness is defined by more subtle valleys, meadows and deep box canyons — prime roaming ground for the estimated 40 or so grizzly bears known to inhabit the region. The terrain is cut by numerous streams and covered with thick forests that yield few recognizable landmarks. Unlike the eastern half, the trails receive scant use and can be easily confused with game trails. Old blazes cut into the trees by army troops almost one hundred years ago are helpful in keeping yourself oriented in the western reaches, particularly across large meadows where trails have already been reclaimed by lack of consistent use. Don't be surprised if the clearly marked trail on your USGS map can not be found on the ground!

Roughly 500 miles of trails bisect Teton Wilderness, most following streams. Horsepacking outfitters are the main users, accounting for over three-fourths of the backcountry traffic. The horses bring nasty, biting flies, adding to the summer hordes of mosquitos. Their impact is minimized if you wear long-sleeve, lightweight shirts and long pants instead of shorts.

One of the prettiest seasons in Teton Wilderness is early fall, but it is best avoided by hikers. From mid-September on, hunting season in one of the most famous big game areas in the country is underway. This is when the trails receive their heaviest use by outfitters and are busiest. A far bigger concern, however, is the danger of your movement being mistaken for that of an animal. If you do chose to venture into the wilderness during hunting season, be sure to wear bright-colored clothing and make a fair amount of noise.

July is the month of choice for myself. Statistically it is the driest and the mountain wildflowers are at their best. Early in that month the snow has left most of the trails but a pretty frosting remains on the higher peaks. Even though visitation in Jackson Hole is at its peak, I rarely see another vehicle at the trailhead parking areas, much less someone on the trail.

For information on the trails contained in this section, other routes, and rules and regulations of the wilderness contact:

Bridger-Teton National Forest
Buffalo Ranger District
Box 278
Moran, Wyoming 83013
307-543-2386

46 BOX CREEK TRAIL

Distance:
 5.3 miles one-way
Elevation gain:
 860 ft.
Elevation loss:
 520 ft.
Maximum elevation:
 8,600 ft.
Maps:
 Rosies Ridge
 Gravel Mountain

The Box Creek Trail is an unsigned spur off the Enos Lake Trail. It offers no bold views or grand scenic statements enroute. It is included in this book because it provides the most direct access to an area struck by a high-altitude tornado.

That rare event occurred on July 21, 1987. According to the Forest Service, the massive twister—believed to be the highest elevation tornado ever recorded—leveled trees along a path 20 miles long and up to two miles wide. Winds were estimated up to 200 miles per hour. Over 14,000 acres of lodgepole and fir were toppled and tossed about like matchsticks. Some trails in the area were permanently closed. It took Forest Service crews—supplemented by volunteer work crews from conservation organizations—four years to finish clearing and re-routing sections of trails. Today, it is interesting to walk through the after effects of the maelstrom, clearly seen along the trail.

To reach the trailhead, drive 30 miles north of Jackson on U.S. Hwy. 89/191 to Moran Junction. There, pass the turnoff to Grand Teton National Park and head east towards Dubois on U.S. Hwy. 26/287. Three-and-a-half miles past the junction, turn left unto the signed Buffalo Valley Road. Drive approximately nine miles to the signed Box Creek Trailhead access road on your left. It is .7 miles to the parking area at the end of the rough road. (Note: The trailhead has been relocated since the 1965 Rosies Ridge topo map was drawn. The map shows the trailhead starting roughly a mile to the west. Although you can still begin there, mileage and description of his hike begin at the new trailhead.)

The trail begins climbing immediately through sagebrush and grass covered hills intermittently shaded by first aspen, then fir and pine trees. Stay to your right where the trail coming in from the old trailhead leads off to the left. At one mile, you'll pass a weathered wood sign marking the Teton Wilderness Boundary. The trail continues climbing at an easy grade along a double dirt track, testimony to its use by outfitters. Soon, it levels and crosses open meadows, where there are nice vistas of the Buffalo River Valley. The forested highlands surrounding Mt. Leidy are seen to your left (S). The trail gently climbs and drops through a boggy area before reaching a meadow bordered by dead snags at 2.4 miles.

After crossing a creek .4 miles further, it ascends to a long, rolling meadow awash with color in midsummer. At 3.6 miles, you reach a poorly signed junction, marked only by a wood sign that says "trail." Go right to reach Enos Lake. To access the unmarked Box Creek Trail and view a segment of the blowdown, continue straight. Cross a creek and head towards the high meadows to your right. The trail ascends 600 feet up the open slopes of Gravel Ridge to a crest of the same, reached at 4.6 miles. Here you are treated to expansive views of the wild, wooded country that defines the Teton Wilderness.

From the ridge the trail swings left and begins to descend the east side of Gravel Ridge. At 11 o'clock ahead of you, you can glimpse the edge of the blowdown. The trail crosses numerous wooden bridges over creek beds/boggy area—all dry the summer of 1995—and eventually connects with the Lava Creek trail at 5.8 miles. Less than a mile from the crest, at 5.3 miles, you are into the blowdown.

The blowdown area along Box Creek trail.

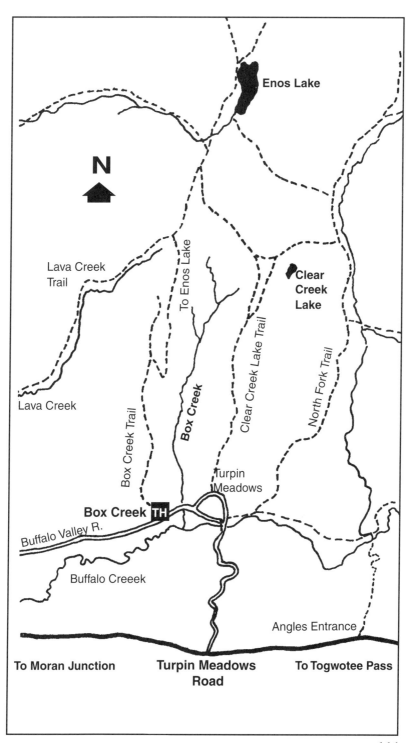

47 ENOS LAKE

Distance:
 11 miles one-way
Elevation gain:
 1,980 ft.
Elevation loss:
 640 ft.
Maximum elevation:
 8,320 ft.
 Rosies Ridge
 Gravel Mountain

Cradled between two spruce-covered and meadowed ridges, deep blue Enos Lake is a popular destination for outfitters who can easily cover the 11 mile distance. Enos is the largest lake in vast Teton Wilderness. Despite soft mud shores and an influx of Utah chubs, it offers reasonably good fishing—as do the numerous creeks In the vicinity, notably Pacific Creek.

To reach the trailhead, drive 30 miles north of Jackson on U.S. Hwy. 89/191 to Moran Junction. There, pass the turnoff to Grand Teton National Park and head east towards Dubois on U.S. Hwy. 26/287. Three-and-a-half miles past the junction, turn left unto the signed Buffalo Valley Road.

Drive approximately nine miles to the signed Box Creek Trailhead access road on your left. It is .7 miles to the parking area at the end of the rough road. (Note: The trailhead has been relocated since the 1965 Rosies Ridge topo map was drawn. The map shows the trailhead starting roughly a mile to the west. Although you can still begin there, mileage and description of his hike begin at the new trailhead.)

The trail begins climbing immediately through sagebrush and grass covered hills intermittently shaded by first aspen, then fir and pine trees. Stay to your right where the trail coming in from the old trailhead leads off to the left. At one mile, you'll pass a weathered wood sign marking the Teton Wilderness Boundary. The trail continues climbing at an easy grade along a double dirt track, testimony to its use by outfitters. Soon, it levels and crosses open meadows, where nice vistas of the Buffalo River Valley and the forested highlands surrounding Mt. Leidy are seen to your left (S). It then gently climbs and drops through a boggy area before reaching a meadow bordered by dead snags at 2.4 miles.

After crossing a creek .4 miles further, it climbs to a long, rolling meadow awash with color in midsummer. At 3.6 miles, you reach a poorly signed junction, marked only by a wood sign that says "trail." Go right to reach Enos Lake.

At the junction, the trail turns sharply south for .4 miles and hugs the base of Gravel Ridge. It then turns north and steeply climbs 260 feet up the same, opening up views of Gravel Mountain to the west and Box Creek Canyon and the Absorakas beyond it to the east. It gradually descends the ridge and enters a long meadow at 5 miles, then hops a tributary of Box Creek .4 miles further and proceeds northeast over relatively flat terrain to a sketchy intersection with Lava Creek Trail at 7 miles. The faint crossroads to your left (W) is identified by a small wood sign near the base of a tree.

Continue straight, dropping steeply then more gradually as your traverse two narrow meadows and a small canyon to reach the intersection with Divide Creek Trail at 8.5 miles This intersection is well-signed. Stay to the left here. The trail to Enos climbs 200 feet out of the canyon and enters the meadows south of the lake, where the trail forks again. Take the right fork, a level walk through flowered fields that crosses the outflow of the lake near the patrol cabin at 9.6 miles. Here, the trail climbs up a ridge above the west side of the lake then drops to its north shore, which offers the best camping spots around the lake.

The body of water and creek are named in honor of John Enos, Chief Washakie's Shoshone cousin. Enos worked as a guide for both Bonneville and Fremont in the early 1800s. In 1915, at the age of 102, he was presented at the San Francisco Exposition. He died four yeas later at the age of 106. He often camped at the lake that now bears his name.

Vast Teton Wilderness, seen from Gravel Ridge.

48 SOUTH FORK FALLS

Distance:
   10.5 miles one-way
Elevation gain:
   620 ft.
Elevation loss:
   1,700 ft.
Maximum elevation:
   8,520 ft.
Maps:
   Angle
   Togwotee

South Fork Falls has my vote for the most spectacular waterfall in Bridger-Teton National Forest. The six-foot wide South Buffalo Fork, squeezed into slot half that size by a large rock pillar, rushes towards the lip of a sheer-walled, narrow chasm and dives over 80 feet straight down to its moss covered bottom.

The impressive falls is reached via a long trek through the southern reaches of Teton Wilderness, limiting most traffic to outfitters and backpackers. Ambitious, fit hikers can do the hike in a long day but will wish they had camped: The trail continues to pretty Ferry Lake and its outlet falls before joining the Soda Fork Trail. This is a superb, 40-mile loop trip if you shuttle a car between Togwotee Lodge and Turpin Meadows.

The hike to the falls may be started from Turpin Meadows or the Angles Entrance to Teton Wilderness behind Togwotee Lodge, the option described below.

Drive north out of Jackson on U.S. Hwy. 89/191 to Moran Junction. Drive past the junction, heading east on U.S. 26/287 towards Dubois. Sixteen miles beyond the junction, you'll see Togwotee Lodge on your right. Turn into the parking lot and follow the dirt road on the left (W) end of the lodge. Stay right when the road forks and drive to the developed trailhead parking area, reached in another .2 miles.

The trail heads north through forest for .4 miles, then begins a steady, steep, switchbacking 1,520 foot descent to the South Buffalo Fork, reached at 2.4 miles. A good bridge spans the river. (A signed short-cut trail is passed at the two mile mark. This up-and-down path through the woods cuts the distance by 1.5 miles, but requires an icy ford of the river, often difficult to negotiate safely until late summer.)

Cross the bridge and ascend 200 feet to a lodgepole-covered bench

South Fork Falls drops more than 80 feet into the Buffalo Fork.

above the river. Hop a small stream at 3.9 miles as the scenic canyon, here lined with berry bushes, begins to narrow. The trail climbs another 180 feet then drops back down to South Buffalo Fork and traverses the base of steep, rocky cliffs.

At 7.1 miles, it enters long, flat Terrace Meadows. To your left (N), 10,258 foot Terrace Mountain rises in steps, giving the mountain its name. The limestone cliffs to your right (S) hide Holmes Cave, described in hike no. 49.

The path re-enters the trees at 8.8 miles. A half-mile further you pass a signed junction to Cub Creek on your right. Continue straight and steeply climb 200 feet up switchbacks. At the top of the climb, a faint but signed trail to your left leads to Nowlin Meadows and the Soda Fork Trail, reached in 5.5 miles. Stay on the main trail. Watch for an unsigned trail to your right in another .3 miles. This is the spur trail that leads to the South Buffalo Fork Gorge and South Fork Falls, 10.5 miles from the trailhead. At the lip of the gorge, turn left and walk up canyon for the best view of the falls.

49 HOLMES CAVE

Distance:
    8.8 miles RT
Elevation gain:
    1,500 ft.
Elevation loss:
    680 ft.
Maximum elevation:
    10,040 ft.
Maps:
    Angle Mtn.
    Togwotee Pass

The hike to Holmes Cave is one of my favorite Jackson Hole excursions. It takes you into the heart of fabulous pinnacle terrain at the north end of the valley. The vast expanse of rolling open meadow colored with red foliage and surprising patches of late-blooming lupine in early fall brings hikers back every September—unless they are lured there in the summer months to catch the height of the wildflower bloom. And, yes, there is an interesting cave at the end of the walk. Holmes is one of the largest caverns in northwest Wyoming, extending over 4,000 feet underground.

To reach the trailhead, drive 30 miles north from Jackson on U.S. 89/191 to Moran Junction. Set your odometer here as you continue straight (E) on U.S. 26/287 towards Dubois. Twenty miles from the junction, immediately beyond a highway speed limit sign, is an unmarked dirt turn-off on the left. Turn in here and drive .1 miles to an obvious parking area on your right. Walk up the badly rutted road, soon passing a small cabin. Left of and beyond it is a small wood sign that reads "Holmes Cave." This is the start of the hike.

The clear trail—not plotted on the topo maps—climbs through scattered forest, gaining approximately 400 feet before dropping slightly to cross an unnamed tributary of Blackrock Creek. It climbs above the creek, recrossing it again at 1.6 miles. Here, the trail parallels the tributary as it begins a sustained, steep climb up a draw, gaining almost 500 feet in the next half mile. At 2.6 miles, you'll pass a wilderness boundary sign. The trail continues its ascent for another .2 miles, reaching the hike's high point of 10,040 feet at an obvious ridge crest.

From the crest it descends to a large cairn and disappears. Walk to the far right—almost due east—and head towards the trees below you. You'll pass two more cairns as you drop 440 feet to the meadow. If you keep right, you'll soon see the trail again.

At 3.6 miles, hop a stream and begin a short but moderately steep climb

The pinnacles near Togwotee are showcased on the hike to Holmes Cave.

The wet entrance to Holmes Cave. Inside is a 31-foot waterfall.

up a wooded draw. The trail switchbacks once before leveling and skirting the right side of an unnamed lake at 4 miles then a small pond just beyond it.

Shortly past the pond, the trail divides. To reach Holmes Cave, take the left fork. Descend 200 feet into a large depression. Water from the entire area drains into this sink hole—the entrance to Holmes Cave. Head towards an obvious, 20 foot high, rock-covered hillside ahead of you. The entrance is at its foot.

Holmes Cave extends approximately 4,000 feet underground. It was discovered by Edwin Holmes from Massachusetts, John Holland from Ohio, and Neil Matheson of Wyoming, in September of 1898. The labyrinth was explored seven years later, September 6-9, 1905, by T.R. Wilson of Afton, Wyoming, and two others. They named its two large rooms Holland and Wilson. Holland, the largest chamber, is 754 feet long and 452 feet wide. (A third chamber, Neda, has since been discovered.)

The cave was explored again in July of 1933. One of the participants, Esther Allen, described the chilly spelunking expedition in an unpublished history of Bridger-Teton National Forest:

"We had to crawl through a small stream that came out of the small entrance to enter a tunnel inside. Through the arrow-shaped hall entry, we passed over ground to the 31-foot waterfall which descended into the Holland Chamber...."

An expedition two months later in August of 1933 determined that the breccia formation was an extinct volcano.

Looking right (NE) from the cave entrance, one can discern a faint trial heading towards a small saddle. From the saddle, the trail descends 200 feet to a small stream. From here, it is possible to walk up 9,910 foot Simpson Peak.

50 ARIZONA CREEK

Distance:
>8.5 miles one-way

Elevation gain:
>1,480 ft.

Maximum elevation:
>8,280 ft.

Maps:
>Huckleberry Mountain
>Colter Bay

Arizona Creek is undoubtedly one of the least-used, wildest places to hike in Jackson Hole. It begins in Grand Teton National Park and soon crosses into the Teton Wilderness. Only several miles from the trailhead, your chances of seeing other people are slim: possibilities of seeing wildlife—even bears—are good. A side trip up nearby Kitten Ridge affords good views of Jackson Lake and the peaks at the north end of the range.

The trailhead to this hike is unsigned. Drive north from Jackson on U.S. 89/191 for 30 miles to Moran Junction. Turn left and drive on U.S. 89/287 for 10 miles to the turn-off to Colter Bay Village. Check your odometer here: the faint, unsigned dirt road to the Arizona Creek traihead turns right off the main highway 4.8 miles beyond the turn-off to Colter Bay Village. The road begins immediately after crossing the bridge over Arizona Creek, also unmarked. Watch closely. The dirt road ends in roughly 300 feet at an old, unused corral where a large log blocks further motorized travel. The topo map shows the road continuing for about a mile, but since the road has been unused for a number of years and was only sparsely traveled before that, it has already been reclaimed by ground vegetation.

Park and walk along the faint roadway to a second corral about 150 feet north. An unmarked path on the corral's left side leads into the woods, cutting through a patch of lodgepole forest before entering Bailey Meadows. This large, rarely visited expanse of grasses and wildflowers is fed by Arizona Creek, Bailey Creek, and numerous unnamed streams flowing down from 9,177 foot Kitten Ridge to the east.

The trail traverses the length of the meadow before climbing a small, aspen-covered hill and dropping down to Arizona Creek at 1.5 miles. Moose, elk and deer are frequently spotted amongst the scattered forest and meadowland near the meandering creek's banks. Bear, including grizzlies, have been reported in this area. It would be wise to make noise as you proceed.

At 2.2 miles, you'll pass the metal stake marking the boundary between Grand Teton National Park and the

Teton Wilderness area of Bridger-Teton National Forest. Shortly after the boundary marking you'll come to an unsigned trail to your left. This has been created by people fishing a side stream and dead-ends in a mile or so in a box canyon. Stay on the main trail, to the right, and begin ascending a wooded ridge that rises roughly 700 feet before topping out at a second meadow fed by Bailey Creek. The right-hand side of the meadow is bounded by Kitten Ridge. A steep but worthwhile cross-country detour to the top of this offers great views of the Teton Range and Jackson Lake.

The main trail bisects the meadow, fording Bailey Creek and heading north to the forest at its far end. It climbs gently out of the meadow before dropping 300 feet to the second crossing of Arizona Creek at 6.5 miles. The last two miles of the trail are often muddy, as it lies at the bottom of the northwest slopes of 9,693 foot Wildcat Peak. You'll cross numerous streams and game trails as you begin the steep, 500 foot climb to the edge of Brown's Meadows and the headwaters of Arizona Creek.

The trail ends at these meadows, which are prime elk grazing habitat. Here you may pick up a trail north to Huckleberry Mountain, or return to the park road via the Pilgrim Creek Trail. Either option would involve a car shuttle beforehand.

Arizona Creek, peak, lake and island are all named after Arizona George, a trapper found dead in this creek in 1888 by his partner, Dog-Faced Pete. Cause of death is unknown. Likewise, Brown's Meadows was also named after an early trapper who was found frozen to death at the headwaters of Arizona Creek.

It is not uncommon to see bears up little-traveled Arizona Creek.

51 HUCKLEBERRY MOUNTAIN

Distance:
   12 miles RT
Elevation gain:
   2,615 ft.
Maximum elevation:
   9,615 ft.
Maps:
   Huckleberry Mountain

As a former U.S. Army administration site, fire lookout station, and location of hideout cabins for the notorious elk tusk hunters at the turn of the century, the area around Huckleberry Mountain is rich in local history. That, plus superb views of the northern end of the Teton Range and southern end of Yellowstone National Park make this destination an engaging choice—not to mention the opportunity to feast on the copious huckleberries that give the ridge its name! Be sure to take suitable containers if you are going in late summer so you can transport the ripe fruit home with you.

From Jackson drive north on U.S. Hwy. 89/191 for 30 miles to Moran Junction. Turn left unto U.S. Hwy. 89/287 and drive another 22 miles to a dirt road off the right-hand side of the highway, located just before the bridge crossing the Snake River near Flagg Ranch.

The dirt road ends at the trailhead after .3 miles. Although called Sheffield Creek Trail on the topo map, the trail sign and common usage identify the trail as Huckleberry Ridge. At the sign you immediately ford shallow Sheffield Creek then walk along an old jeep trail a short distance to a fork. Stay right, heading through a small meadow to a second sign. Beyond this you'll begin a steady climb up Huckleberry Ridge, ascending continuously for over 1,600 feet before finally dipping across the headwaters of Sheffield Creek. The downhill respite is short, as the trail soon resumes its upward course through scattered forest and open slopes for another 600 feet to the top of the ridge at 9,200 feet. Over seven miles in length, the ridge extends from Arizona Creek north towards Yellowstone with fine views of the Teton Range and the southern end of Yellowstone's high plateaus and canyons. It's high point is 9,615 foot Huckleberry Mountain, reached by following the trail to Rodent Creek. Pass a turn-off to the left (an unofficial trail that short-cuts to Rodent Creek) and walk a short way to a trail on the right that leaves the main route. This short spur trail climbs 400 feet to the top of Huckleberry Mountain, where there is an abandoned fire lookout station on top that is fun to explore.

Huckleberry Ridge was originally called "Soldier's Hill," as it was used as a lookout point by U.S. Army troops before the formation of the National Park Service in 1916. In 1938, CCC crews constructed a 15x17 foot, two-story fire lookout tower on the ridge. The bottom floor, constructed of locally obtained logs, was used for storage. The upper story was used to survey the predominantly lodgepole forest at the northern end of the forest and Grand Teton and Yellowstone National parks. Two hundred panes of glass wrap around all four sides of this level, accessed outside by a log staircase. The cement, hardware, shingles, glass and other materials for the structure were packed in by mules.

Huckleberry was one of six lookouts the CCC's built on the northern half of the forest in the 1930s. The others were strategically located at Deer Creek, Munger Mountain, Baldy Mountain, Signal Mountain and Blacktail Butte. Changing fire policies, reporting done by public and private aircraft, and more efficient detection methods eventually made the lookout towers obsolete. Huckleberry was last used as an active lookout the summer of 1957.

When the Forest Service began to dismantle the lookouts, protection was sought for the two-story structure. In 1980, Bridger-Teton Recreation Staff Officer Bob Perkins wrote in a nomination form for historic site designation that the Huckleberry Lookout "is a significant example of rustic design employed by the United States Forest Service and built by the Civilian Conservation Corps during the first half of this century."

The U. S. Department of Interior granted historic designation, and the building was placed on the National Register of Historic Places. It is the only lookout still standing on the northern portion of the forest. Six lookouts—in various states of disrepair—still stand on the southern half of the forest. (See hike no. 73 to Elk Mountain).

At the turn of the century—well before the lookout tower was built—Huckleberry Ridge was the site of hideout cabins for notorious elk tuskers William Binkley, Charles Isabel and Charles Purdy. The BPOE (Elk's Club) formerly used the animal's canine teeth, or tusks, as its insignia, unintentionally fostering illegal poaching. At the time the tusks could fetch as much as $100, making it a financially lucrative activity. The trio slaughtered thousands of elk—leaving their carcasses behind and only removing the eye teeth—before game wardens were finally able to apprehend and prosecute Binkley and Purdy in 1907. Each were sentenced to three-month terms at the army guardhouse at Mammoth in Yellowstone National Park. Isabel was never apprehended.

TOGWOTEE PASS
▲

Across the Great Divide is a phase aptly suited to Togwotee Pass, the eastern entrance to Jackson Hole. The tree-lined road separates the Absaroka Mountain Range to the north from the Wind River Range to the south. Its 9,658 foot highpoint sits astride the Continental Divide, and is the boundary between Brider-Teton National Forest to the west and Shoshone National Forest to the east.

Used for hundreds of years by Indians traveling from the Wind River Valley into Jackson Hole, the first white men to discover the natural route were John Hoback, Edward Robinson and Jacob Reznor in 1810. Most of the early trappers and explorers, however, seemed unaware of its existence.

The natural divide was officially mapped by Capt. William A. Jones of the U.S. Engineering Corps in 1873. Jones was sent to the region to survey a route for a possible army road into Yellowstone National Park, which had been created by Congress only a year earlier. He hired a Sheepeater Indian medicine man named Togwotee as one of his guides, and subsequently named the pass after him. Togwotee is a Shoshone word with two meanings. One is "lance thrower." The second, more literal translation, is, "to see anywhere from here" or "to go anywhere from here," a fitting description of the feeling one gets when dropping into Jackson Hole from the top of the pass.

A military road over the pass was not constructed until 1898. It passed just outside of Dubois to the Buffalo Fork. Two years later it was extended to the northern end of Jackson Lake. A rough mud affair that was little more than a wagon road, it was not crossed by automobile until 1916. In response to the urging of Lander and Casper residents eager to develop Yellowstone tourism, Wyoming Governor Carey acquired funds from the National Park Service to improve the route over the pass in 1921.

The hikes in this section are in the southern end of the Absaroka Range off the north side of the road. All explore the beautiful breccia pinnacles rising thousands of feet above lakes and mountains at their base. These colorful, banded cliffs are the eroded remains of volanic layers sculpted by wind and water into striking monuments. Compared to the Tetons the area receives little visitation. It is administered by the Wind River Ranger District of Bridger-Teton National Forest. For further information, call or write:

>Bridger-Teton National Forest
>Wind River Ranger District
>Box 186
>Dubois, Wyoming 82513
>307-455-2465

52 JADE LAKE

Distance:
  5 miles RT
Elevation gain:
  432 ft.
Maximum elevation:
  9,532 ft.
Maps:
  Togwotee Pass

Dropping down Togwotee Pass towards Dubois, motorists are treated to one of the most stunning roadside panoramas in the west — a two-mile stretch of volcanic cliffs and pinnacles that shoot into the sky. The deep green waters of Upper and Lower Jade Lakes in the Absorkas reflect these multi-colored banded formations and surrounding countryside beautifully. This is one of the most rewarding short hikes in the region, and unlike Hidden Falls in neighboring Grand Teton National Park, it gets very few visitors.

The trail to the lakes begins at the parking area near Brooks Lake campground. Drive 30 miles north of Jackson on U.S. 89/191 to Moran Junction. There, pass the turnoff to Grand Teton National Park and head east towards Dubois on U.S. Hwy 26/287. Roughly 30 miles from the junction you'll see a signed road that turns off the left-hand side of the highway to Brooks Lake Lodge. Follow the road 5.2 miles to the parking area just past the Brooks Lake Campground.

The trail begins as a jeep track around the south side of Brooks Lake, narrowing then forking in a half mile, with the right fork going towards Upper Brooks Lake and the towering breccia cliffs two miles distant. To reach Jade lakes, veer left (NW) and walk up one of the eroded, parallel trails scarring the hillside. The numerous paths merge into one as the gradient eases, entering a lodgepole pine forest roughly a mile from the trailhead. You then wind slightly uphill through the trees until you reach the emerald waters of Upper Jade Lake one mile further. Don't be disappointed by the small, scummy green pond encountered a half-mile before the lake and turn around — it's not Upper Jade!

The volcanic cliffs and pinnacles that rise over 2,000 feet above the lake are best reflected in the mirror-like stillness of dawn and dusk, times you are also most likely to see wildlife coming to the lakeshore to drink. Good camping sites are found near the lake's outlet on the northern shore and on its southwestern shore. Lower Jade Lake lies another half mile to the northeast. While it lacks the stunning reflections found in Upper Jade's still waters, the peaceful lake offers both good fishing and seclusion.

53 UPPER BROOKS & RAINBOW LAKE

Distance:
   Upper Brooks: 7 miles RT
   Rainbow Lake: 8.2 miles RT
Elevation gain:
   120 ft.
Maximum Elevation:
   9,220 ft.
Maps:
   Togwotee Pass

No grunt climbs up Teton-size hills. No people wearing T-shirts that say "I survived" anything. Great fishing. Beautiful scenery. Run that list of requirements past any number of locals and they may start humming "To dream, the impossible dream..." Yet such a place exists only an hour from downtown Jackson: Upper Brooks and Rainbow Lakes.

The trail to the lakes begins at the parking area near Brooks Lake Campground. Drive 30 miles north of Jackson on U.S. 89/191 to Moran Junction. There, pass the turnoff to Grand Teton National Park and head east towards Dubois on U.S. Hwy 26/287. Roughly 30 miles from the junction you'll see a signed road that turns off the left-hand side of the highway to Brooks Lake Lodge. Follow the road 5.2 miles to the parking area just past the Brooks Lake Campground.

The trail begins as a jeep track around the south side of Brooks Lake, narrowing then forking in a half mile. Stay right. A half-mile ahead at a trail junction, stay right (NE). The trail wanders through meadows sprinkled with purple asters, scarlet paintbrush, yellow cinquefoil and buttercups, violet elephanthead, indigo forget-me-nots and many other wildflowers that will have you flipping madly through your field guides for identification. It's a veritable natural garden that hits its peak bloom in mid-summer, fed by the three or four small tributaries you splash through as you hike beyond Brooks Lake. Splash is the correct word: all but one are too wide to jump across. The abundant water makes this an excellent breeding ground for mosquitos; be sure to bring repellent for this hike.

Near the northern end of Lower Brooks Lake you climb up a short, steep hillside, virtually the only noticeable grade on the whole trip. Thick conifers block the view to the left, but straight ahead and to your right (N and E) the colorful volcanic cliffs above Bonneville Creek and jagged outcroppings of Pinnacle Buttes slice the sky, some almost 12,000 feet high. The trail stays atop a gentle, grassy ridge between two shallow drainages. At the two mile mark it swings to the right and crosses Brooks Lake Creek before entering the trees. Shortly, you'll pass the Bonneville Pass Trail on your right, incorrectly shown on both the USGS quad and the Shoshone Forest Service map as being nearer Brooks Lake. Stay on the main trail, crossing several small tributaries as the trail wanders in-and-out of trees and high meadows.

At 2.9 miles, you'll get your first view of Upper Brooks Lake. The trail crosses two branches of the creek at 3.1 miles then heads right, skirting the east side of the lake. Good campsites are found all around the lake. To gain access to the best sites, follow the trail to the north side of Upper Brooks.

Although the topo map does not show it, a less developed trail loops all the way around the northern end of the lake then follows the creek's west tributary to Rainbow Lake at 4.1 miles. Visited almost solely by fishermen, this lake offers both seclusion and nice camping areas.

Those desiring a longer outing can continue on the trail past Upper Brooks Lake to Bear Cub Pass, three-quarters of a mile beyond the northern end of the lake. Little more than a wooded hilltop, the pass marks the boundary between Shoshone National Forest and Teton Wilderness. From the pass the trail drops two miles to Cub Creek drainage, an infrequently visited but beautiful area.

Plan a stop at Brooks Lake Lodge on your return to the parking lot. The impressive structure, built in 1922 by Eugene Amoretti of Lander, is on the National Register of Historic Places. During the summer months it is open to the general public on Saturdays. At its heyday the lodge provided accommodations for travelers enroute from Lander to Yellowstone National Park. When improved automotive technology enabled them to comfortably cover more ground, business at the log hostelry declined. Its owners tried to revive the operation by converting the lodge into a dude ranch, the Diamond G. The ranch went through a series of owners and a name change through the 40s and 50s before it was closed for a period of time. In 1983, a Minnesota doctor purchased the property and succeeded in having it placed on the historic register, a designation that enabled him to receive federal restoration funds to repair the lodge. The Carlsburg family purchased the property in 1987, completed extensive renovation work, and re-opened it to the public.

The lodge, creek and lakes are named in honor of Bryant Brooks, governor of Wyoming from 1905 to 1911.

▲

54 KISINGER LAKES LOOP

Distance:
 17.4 mile loop
Elevation gained:
 1,240 ft.
Maximum Elevation:
 10,080 ft.
Maps:
 Togwotee Pass
 Dundee Meadows
 Kisinger Lakes

The Kisinger Lakes loop could be done in one long day. It is best done in two to allow time to enjoy the unique DuNoir area of Shoshone National Forest. Four clear lakes reflecting jagged breccia pinnacles, an impressive cirque, continuous stretches of dense forest and wonderful solitude await the backpacker on this trip. The loop starts around Brooks Lake, travels over Bonneville Pass via the DuNoir Trail, joins the Kisinger Lakes Trail, and returns to Brooks Lake by the Pinnacle Trail.

To reach the trailhead, drive 30 miles north of Jackson on U.S. Hwy. 89/191 to Moran junction. Pass the turn-off to Grand Teton National Park and head east towards Dubois on U.S. Hwy 26/287. Approximately 27 miles from the junction, turn left onto the signed Forest Service Road to Brooks Lake Lodge. Follow the road 5.2 miles to the lakeshore parking area past Brooks Lake Campground. The trail begins as a jeep track that circles the south side of the lake.

At a half-mile, the trail forks left towards Jade Lake. Stay right and continue around the lake, climbing a short, steep hill at its northern end. Here you'll enjoy a magnificent view of jagged Pinnacle Butte ahead of you as you gradually ascend a grassy ridge. You'll cross Brooks Lake Creek at two miles and shortly reach the signed turn-off to Bonneville Pass on your right. This is incorrectly shown on old topo maps as being closer to Lower Brooks Lake; it is actually nearer Upper Brooks.

The next two miles of trail climb gradually through pleasant forests and glades, crossing and recrossing Bonneville Creek. To your left an unnamed 10,821 foot peak rises almost 1,500 feet above the draw. Jules Bowl is on the right. This memorable cirque has a relatively flat headwall in the middle and the craggy spires of Pinnacle Butte on the right and left.

At 4.5 miles you reach the western end of Bonneville Pass, a 10,000 ft., half-mile long meadow that gradually drops towards the northeast. A small lake on the pass, source of Dundee Creek, is a nice spot to camp or stop for lunch. The trail follows the outlet to the far end of the meadow, where it drops over 1,000 feet down a steep draw to Dundee Meadows at six miles.

Passing through the meadows the trail forks at 6.8 miles, heading left (E) to Murray and Clendenning Lakes. Stay right, crossing West DuNoir Creek and its tributaries three times before beginning a gradual 400 foot climb to Basin Creek Meadows at 9.2 miles. Fed by two springs that form the creek, the meadows offer a nice place to camp. Kisinger Lakes lie just .4 miles further, but their shores tend to be marshy and not as desirable for an overnight stay. The pretty lakes do provide a perfect mirror for Pinnacle Butte rising sharply to the west. Plan on being at the lakes at dusk to catch the rosy alpenglow on the rocky spires, the highest 11,516 feet.

The trail heads south from the lakes, cutting through the center of the cluster and rounding the southeast side of the butte before reaching the sign for Pinnacle Trail at 11.6 miles. The "trail" is nowhere to be seen, since it crosses a small overgrown meadow. Turn right at the sign and head northwest towards the base of the butte, climbing about 200 feet as you round it's corner. Here you'll clearly see Pinnacle Trail. The path gradually descends 4.5 miles to Brooks Lake Road, 16.6 miles from the start of the loop. The easy walk goes through dense forest, crossing numerous streams tumbling down the west side of the butte. Unfortunately, the thoroughly enjoyable hike ends in an old clearcut just before reaching the road, breaking the spell woven by the woods. Turn right at the road and walk the .8 miles back to your car.

Dundee Meadows is a wild garden of flowers.

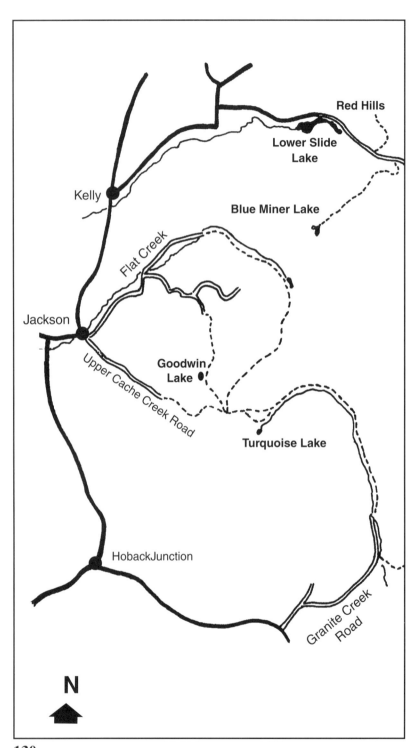

THE GROS VENTRE

▲

The east side of Jackson Hole is defined by the Gros Ventre Mountain Range, a rugged, weathered group of sedimentary peaks that run northwest to southeast. A dozen summits surpass the 10,000 foot mark; an additonal eight top 11,000 feet. Sheep Mountain and Pyramid Peak dominate the northwest end; Doubletop Peak, the highest in the range at 11,682 feet, rises near the eastern end.

First included in Teton Forest Reserve in 1897 and later in Teton National Forest in 1908, the bulk of the 300,000 acre range was placed under wilderness protection in October of 1984 when Congress enacted the Wyoming Wilderness Act. Wilderness designation protects the resource from both timbering and mining activity. The latter played a noteworthy part in the range's natural history. Coal was discovered near the upper end of Slide Lake in 1890. Two years later local businessmen formed the Jackson Hole Coal Company and began digging a 60-foot tunnel to access the 15-foot long vein. The mayor of Jackson burned the first lumps from the venture in 1924, but transportation problems prevented it from being more widely extracted. In more recent years oil and gas exploration and pressure from timbering companies, many of whom have since closed or moved away, made passage of the wilderness bill a political dogfight.

Luckily, conservationists prevailed. The largely-intact range is home to large numbers of elk, deer, moose, bighorn sheep, and the occasional black bear. Grizzlies are not known to frequent the range. Over 200 miles of trails rise from the sage-covered valley floor through flower-filled meadows, aspen and lodgepole. Engelmann spruce and alpine fir shade the trails as they near the crest. There are relatively few lakes but numerous streams and waterfalls, including spectacular three-tired Shoal Falls described in this section. Most of the trails are snow-free by late June.

Geologically, the Gros Ventre is a fascinating region. The sedimentary rocks were once the bottom of a long vanished inland sea. Roughly 50 million years ago a major uplift formed the peaks we know today, exposing a panoply of different sediments in the limestone, sandstone and shale that compose the range — nowhere more colorful than the Red and Lavender Hills.

The forces that uplifted the peaks are still active. Less than 70 years ago a sizeable tremor dislodged over fifty million cubic yards of earth and rock from the face of Sheep Mountain, sending it crashing to the bottom of the Gros Ventre River Canyon and 400 feet up the other side in under three minutes. It has been estimated that if the Panama Canal had been excavated at the same rate of speed, the 51-mile trench would have been completed in under one hour. The area, known as the Gros Ventre Slide, can be hiked and is also included in this section.

The Gros Ventres were first visited by Indians following game herds near what is now Pinedale, through the Upper Green River drainage, and across the range into Jackson Hole. French trappers gave the migrants and the range its name in the early 1800s. One account holds that the Indians rubbed their hands over their stomachs to designate their tribal sign of three stripes around their waist. This was misinterpreted by the French as being the sign for the "big bellied" Indians, or "Gros Ventre." A second account believes that when the trappers saw the open canyons of the range, they exclaimed, "Gros Ventre!," or great opening.

To check on trail conditions and obtain a list of the rules and regulations for the wilderness, write or call:

                    Bridger-Teton National Forest
                    Jackson District
                    Box 1689
                    Jackson, Wyoming 83001
                    307-739-5400

55 TOPPINGS LAKES & RIDGE

Distance:
    Toppings Lakes: 5.2 miles RT
    Ridge: 6.4 miles RT
Elevation gain:
    Toppings Lakes: 1,500 ft.
    Ridge: 2,020 ft.
Maximum elevation:
    Toppings Lakes: 8,600 ft.
    Ridge: 9,120 ft.
Maps:
    Davis Hill (Not plotted)
    Mt. Leidy (Not plotted)

If you only have a short morning or an afternoon to hike—or if you are looking for good fishing—Toppings Lakes should be near the top of your prospect list. The two small lakes were stocked with grayling by Fred Toppings, for whom they are named. Fred and Eva started the Moosehead Ranch in the late 1920s. They gradually expanded their small operation, taking in game hunters in the fall and dudes in the summer. The latter were treating to a horseback ride to the lakes.

At its height in the 1960s, Topping's Moosehead Ranch had over 40 cabins, a school, and its own post office, registered under the name of Elk. Both the school and post office were closed by 1969. Fred died in 1970, Eva in 1988. The ranch is still in operation under new owners.

The unmarked trail to the lakes is reached by driving 24.5 miles north of Jackson on U.S. 89/191 to a signed Teton National Forest access road on the right, almost directly opposite the Cunningham Cabin turn-off on the left side of the highway.

Turn right unto the access road. Pass an information kiosk at .7 miles. A short distance further, the road forks, with Road #30310 turning sharply left and Road #30333 continuing straight. Take the left fork. It immediately switchbacks up a steep hill that crests at 1.1 miles.

Stay right at 2.3 miles where a logging road veers left, and drive up the cobbled grade. At 2.9 miles, you'll pass several ponds to your right that are often covered with striking pink algae in mid-summer. Stay right again at 3.2 miles where the road forks. The unimproved dirt road gets progressively rougher, but it is passable in

Lily pads cover the outflow to Toppings Lake.

sedans if you travel slowly and carefully. At 4.7 miles, park in the graveled area to your right. Walk .1 miles up the road to a gate (usually barred). You'll see a wood trail marker but no sign of a trail. The trail begins approximately two minutes up the road on the right-hand side. Look carefully. If you are still on the road as it swings noticeably to the left, you've missed it.

The trail abruptly climbs through lodgepole forest, switchbacking slightly west but heading predominantly southeast through cool woods. Good eyes will spot a wonderful assortment of edible berries in early fall.

Thick foliage hides an intermittent stream to your left—outflow from a pond above you—that parallels the trail. At 1.8 miles, you see the first indication that you are in the right place: a small, wood Forest Service sign that reads "Toppings Lakes." Of course, the sign is right before a junction and it doesn't indicate which way to go! To reach the lakes, descend on the left fork, passing the pond below you before dropping down to a sunny meadow and the first lake. The trail follows its left (N) shore to its outflow and the second, prettier lake, reached 2.6 miles from the trailhead. Look closely at the trees bordering the lake. Old claw marks high on the trunks offer mute evidence that you are in bear country.

Those with time and the inclination will be well rewarded by taking the right fork at the signed junction. This leads to a ridge above the lakes. The trail climbs steeply a half-mile to a ridge. Turning left on the ridge and walking 10 minutes to a high point gains vistas of Mt. Leidy rising above Toppings Lake. Walking right brings you closer to a panoramic view of the Teton Range and Jackson Lake.

56 GROS VENTRE SLIDE

Distance:
    1.6 miles one-way
Elevation gained:
    720 fft.
Maximum elevation:
    7,640 ft.
Maps:
    Shadow Mountain
    Blue Miner Lake

On May 18, 1927, the town of Kelly was destroyed by a tremendous flood that demolished its buildings and claimed six lives. The entire settlement was washed away by a wall of water so large that the town of Wilson, miles away on the other side of the valley, was also submerged under six feet of water before the flood subsided.

The event was the second act of a dramatic geologic play begun two years earlier. The afteroon of June 23, 1925, fifty million cubic yards of dirt and Tensleep sandstone — heavily saturated by rain and loosened by earth tremors — slid off the face of Sheep Mountain. Gaining momentum quickly, the debris swept down the mountain, into the Gros Ventre River Canyon 2,000 feet below, then climbed 400 feet up the other side in under three minutes. The slide formed an earthen dam 225 feet high across the river, completely blocking it's flow and creating what is today called Lower Slide Lake. State surveyors and engineers who subsequently visited the site believed the dam to be permanent. They were wrong. Exceptionally heavy rain and snow in May of 1927 caused the lake to overflow the earthen dam and wash it away, creating the sudden and disastrous flood that decimated Kelly 3.5 miles downstream. Within a matter of hours the level of Lower Slide Lake dropped over 50 feet.

The geologic story is clearly told on a .4 mile interpretative trial constructed by the Forest Service and the YWCA. It is reached by driving north of town on U.S. Hwy 89/191 to the Gros Ventre Junction. Turn right at the junction and drive past the town of Kelly at 7.2 miles to the signed Gros Ventre Road at 8.4 miles. Turn right and drive 4.5 miles to the marked Gros

Ventre Slide Intrepretative Trail pullout.

One of the best ways to comprehend the size of the mile-long, 2,000 foot wide slide is to actually walk in it. This is most easily accomplished by following the main drainage up the slide's face, a difficult but fascinating cross-country route that involves walking through heavy brush and loose talus. To reach the face of the slide, drive 150-200 yards past the interpretative pullout to a dirt road on your right that leads down to the lake. The narrow road crosses the bridge below Lower Slide Lake in a half mile. Turn right unto a jeep trail shortly after crossing the bridge and park. Hike along the jeep trail, staying right of the creek. Then go left towards the drainage when the trail begins to swing right. Climb above the brush on the loose rock, avoiding the steeper slide wall as you work your way up the boulder fields.

Three-quarters of a mile up the slide you'll reach a group of conifers that provide a good stopping point to view this incredible geologic phenomenon.

The drainage can be followed an estimated 1.5 miles to the top of the fracture, a challenging boulder route that should not be attempted by the inexperienced. As an alternate return route, walk west to several small ponds in the middle of the slide path before crossing back to the east side and dropping into the drainage to descend.

Hikers are advised that the terrain and rock on the slide path is unstable and rough. Proceed with appropriate caution.

▲

57 BLUE MINER LAKE & SHEEP MTN.

Distance:
    Blue Miner Lake: 7.5 miles one-way
    Sheep Mtn. via Blue Miner Lake: 10 miles one-way
Elevation gain:
    Blue Miner Lake: 3,370 ft.
    Sheep Mtn. via Blue Miner Lake: 5,170 ft.
Maximum elevation:
    Blue Miner Lake: 9,700 ft.
    Sheep Mountain: 11,239 ft.
Maps:
    Grizzly Lake
    Blue Miner Lake

The Sleeping Indian has slumbered for years just above the town of Kelly. Officially known as Sheep Mountain, it doesn't take much imagination to see the shape of a giant Indian lying down, his stomach and body forming the long, gradual slope of the main peak to the north and his head—with its pointy nose and headdress—being the 11,106 foot subsidiary peak to the south. A scramble to the top of the Indian's belly, the true summit, is blessed with grand views of the valley and the distant snow-covered Wind River Range on the northeast horizon.

Sparkling Blue Miner Lake lies over 1,800 feet below the main summit at the base of the Sleeping Indian, a jewel whose beauty is enhanced by its wild, rugged setting. The hike to the lake gains over 3,000 feet. While it can be done in a long day, the trip is an ideal candidate for a two or three day backpack to allow time to scramble up the Indian and explore the surrounding area.

Drive north of Jackson on U.S. Hwy. 189/191 to Gros Ventre junction. Turn right at the junction and drive past the town of Kelly at 7.2 miles to the signed Gros Ventre Road at 8.4 miles. Turn right and drive 11.5 miles to the new trailhead on the right side of the road, opposite the Red Hills Campground. The new start of the trail adds an additional 400 feet of elevation gain and another mile or so to an already long hike. The Forest Service moved the trailhead because of repeated complaints from nearby private property owners that recreational users were crossing their land—illustrating the growing problem of access to public lands beyond private property.

The new trail heads east up a hill, then turns southwest and climbs it before dropping down to the old trail. After a brief flat stretch, it gently switchbacks up a sage-covered hillside to a blazed tree near its top. Here, the trail curves right through meadow and is occasionally obscure: Look for the blazes to help you stay on course.

At three miles, you'll reach a level contour and head east through meadows and scattered clumps of trees before winding to the right and climbing a ridge. Here, you can gaze into West Miner Creek and Crystal Creek drainages below you.

The distinct trail stays slightly below the ridgetop as it steadily gains elevation. At a blazed arrow it turns left and steeply climbs the next 300 feet to the ridge itself, following it to a point marked on the topo map as "8,947," roughly 4.2 miles from the new trailhead. The Indian dominates the view to the southwest, while the familiar Teton skyline is silhouetted along the northwest horizon.

The trail drops slightly at a saddle before climbing steeply again for another 1.2 miles then swinging left to the edge of a steep drop-off. On a clear day, the jagged peaks of the Wind River Range 50 miles away can be seen to the east-southeast. From this overlook, walk right towards a wildflower-filled clearing and ascend through fir and limber pine to reach an alpine meadow at 5.7 miles.

The trail often fades out along its mile-long path through the grass. Stay towards the middle of the meadow and look for a blazed pine in the left treeline near the meadow's end.

Follow the blazes another half mile to the trees at the edge of the amphitheater above the lake. The high ridge overlooks the often snow-covered cirque above Blue Miner and a startlingly blue, unnamed lake to the southeast locally dubbed "Betty Davis' Eyes."

Continue on the ridge until you reach a cairn marking a route that descends west to Blue Miner Lake 600 feet below you. Campsites can be found on the lake's south and west shores.

The climb up to the belly of the Indian starts from the south shore of the lake. It is a non-technical but steep 1,800 foot scramble up the mountainside. The cirque frequently contains snow until early August. Late season it is usually possible to reach the north ridge of the main summit without crossing significant snowfields.

If you are not dropping to the lake, Sleeping Indian can be climbed by staying on the ridge and walking west. Follow the ridge until it curves south, roughly .4 miles. From here, it is another 1,000 feet and one mile to the Indian's "belly."

▲

58 RED HILLS

Distance:
    4.4 miles RT
Elevation gained:
    1,320 ft.
Maximum elevation:
    8,420 ft.
Maps:
    Grizzly Lake
    Mt. Leidy

A walk to the Red Hills in the Gros Ventre Range northeast of Jackson offers a truly wonderful view of the Tetons, 20 miles distant. From atop a ridge, the range skyrockets above a striking foreground of russet cliffs and slopes that give the surrounding terrain its name.

To reach the trailhead, drive seven miles north of Jackson on U.S. Hwy 89/191 to the Gros Ventre Junction. Turn right (E) and drive 7.2 miles to the town of Kelly. Roughly a mile beyond town you'll see a paved road on the right that leads to Lower Slide Lake. Turn here and drive to the end of the pavement at six miles. Continue on unpaved road for 4.2 miles, just beyond the Red Hills Ranch sign on the right-hand side of the road. This is private property: Please act accordingly. Park off the side of the road, cross it, and head roughly 300 feet right (E) to the start of a distinct but unmarked trail that is not readily apparent from the road. If you drive across the nearby bridge spanning the Gros Ventre River at 10.8 miles you've gone too far. Backtrack a half mile from the bridge and look for the trail.

The trail climbs steeply northeast up a large, unnamed canyon until it crests a treeless ridge at 1.5 miles. The impressive, gray-blue striated Lavender Hills lie to the north. The view offers a good excuse to sit down, catch your breath and have a sip of water. Be sure to bring plenty with you as none is available on the hike. The unshaded ridges can radiate intense heat on hot summer days.

From this ridge, a sketchy trail that is difficult to follow leads to the top of a second ridgetop to the northwest, .7 miles away. When the trail begins to fade, bear slightly to the left and you'll probably be able to pick up its faint outline on the slope ahead of you. If not, walk cross-country through the open terrain.

The view from the top of the second ridge offers one of the prettiest vistas in the entire region, with both the Teton Range and the Red Hills, for which the Gros Ventres are famous, before you. Sunset is a particularly appealing time to be here. The sun lights the Red Hills on fire before slipping behind the Tetons and rimming the peaks in gold.

59 SHOAL FALLS

Distance:
  11.2 miles RT
Elevation gain:
  2,122 ft.
Maximum elevation:
  8,540 ft.
Maps:
  Granite Falls
  Doubletop Peak

One of the valley's first resident physicians was Dr. Don MacLeod, who moved to Jackson Hole in the 1930s. The overworked doctor spent much of his rare time off roaming his beloved Gros Ventre Range. When he retired valley residents successfully lobbied to have a lake east of Granite Hot Springs named MacLeod Lake as a tribute to his service.

Of all the places Doc frequented none was as dear to him as the area around Shoal Falls, which he called "the most beautiful in the entire range." Many who visit it would agree. The emerald green meadows at the base of the falls backdrop a snow-capped line of peaks which form the spine of the Gros Ventre Range, starting with Palmer Peak to the northeast and moving southwest to Triangle Peak, Doubletop Peak, Hodges Peak, Eagle Peak and Tosi Peak.

To reach the trailhead, drive 13 miles south of Jackson on U.S. Hwy. 89/191 to Hoback Junction. Turn left towards Pinedale on U.S. Hwy 189/191 and drive another 11.8 miles down Hoback Canyon to the "Granite Recreation Area" junction on the left-hand side of the highway. Turn in and drive eight miles to the marked Swift Creek Trailhead on the right side of the road. If you pass the turnoff to Granite Creek Campground, you've missed the trailhead and will have to backtrack about a mile.

The narrow, sometimes rutted dirt road to the trailhead crosses a bridge over Granite Creek then swings left at a sign that reads ".5 miles Swift Cr. - Shoal Lake Trail Junction." Look for an off-road parking spot and begin walking up the old road until you reach the motor closure sign. Here, a single path begins to climb gradually, crossing a Granite Ranch culvert and turning right onto the signed Shoal Lake Trail at .2 miles. In another .2 miles turn left at the signed junction and climb up a steep hillside. Ahead is Open Door Pinnacle, an interesting mountain to the north whose south-facing vertical slab appropriately resembles a door left ajar.

Stay left where an unsigned trail drops to Granite Ranch, and continue climbing northeast through forests of first aspen then spruce and fir. The trail opens up to good views of 10,368 foot

The spectacular high country below Shoal Falls in the Gros Ventre Range.

Ramshorn Peak behind you, then bears right and accesses a ridge at two miles.

A gradual climb up the ridge leads you first to a drainage fringed with willows, then an open meadow at 2.5 miles. At the top of the meadow the trail drops down a small bowl and climbs to the top of a second meadow, then descends the steep hillside and gully leading to West Shoal Creek at 3.4 miles.

Cross the creek and stay to the right of a dry bed shown on the topo map as an intermittent stream. The trail gradually climbs the sage-covered drainage for over a mile before coming to a hilltop view of the glaciated face of Palmer peak at 4.5 miles. After dropping down and climbing out of a grassy bowl, another view of the surrounding peaks opens up at five miles. From this point the trail drops northeast over a number of small plateaus to Shoal Creek, 5.6 miles from the trailhead. Just above are three beaver ponds. To get to the spectacular, three-tiered waterfall follow the trail on the east side of the valley for about a quarter of a mile.

Shoal Lake can be reached by following the trail north another 3.1 miles past the falls.

60 TURQUOISE LAKE

Distance:
  11 miles one-way
Elevation gain:
  2,480 ft.
Maximum elevation:
  9,480 ft.
Maps:
  Granite Falls
  Crystal Peak
  Turquoise Lake

Views of sharply glaciated, snow-capped mountains greet hikers enroute to Turquoise Lake, a deep blue-green body of water cradled in a pocket at the base of 11,190 foot Gros Ventre Peak. The trail steadily gains elevation as it climbs through the forests and meadows of lower Granite Creek to the rocky walls of the creek's upper reaches. Hikers can either return the same way or walk 2.2 miles to the top of Cache Creek Pass and descend 6 miles to the valley floor via the Cache Creek Trail.

To reach the trailhead, drive 13 miles south of Jackson on U.S. Hwy. 89/191 to Hoback Junction. There, go left on U.S. Hwy 189/191 towards Pinedale. Drive 11.8 miles to the Granite Creek Recreation Area and turn left at the sign. It is almost 10 miles from the highway to the trailhead parking area at Granite Hot Springs. Be sure to register your vehicle with the attendant at the springs if you plan to leave it in the parking area overnight.

After crossing the Granite Creek footbridge, walk between the hot springs pool and the changing house towards the unmarked but obvious trail. As it gradually climbs through the trees you cross a tributary then small, open meadows before traversing rocky terrain and deadfall. After two miles, the trail climbs to the base of a high ridge connecting Pyramid Peak to the north and Antoinette Peak to the southeast. The left side of the valley is dominated by sheer granite walls breached by meadows and avalanche run-outs at first 2.6 then 2.8 miles. Winding through avalanche debris, talus and sage, pass Bunker Creek drainage at 3.6 miles and continue to gradually ascend.

The grade steepens at four miles as you round a slight rise, pass through two groups of conifers, then skirt a rocky basin at 4.4 miles. Here you'll enjoy your first open vista of the surrounding countryside. The sheer face and lower talus fields of 11,107 foot Pyramid Peak dominates the northern skyline, while an impressive but unnamed rocky peak to the east/southeast catches your attention. As you continue climbing, you'll pass a hunt-

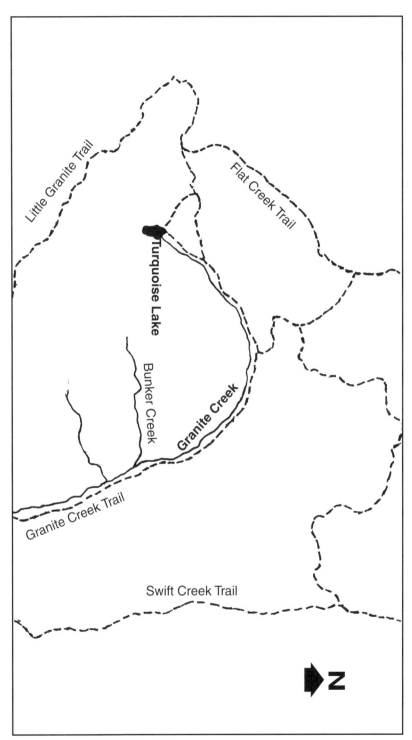

ing camp on the other side of Granite Creek at five miles, then begin angling northwest to an unmarked trail junction at 7.8 miles. The trail to the right heads north, eventually intersecting the Flat Creek Trail. Keep to the left, climbing steadily above the muddy marshland to a second trail fork at 9.8 miles. The right fork leads to Flat Creek Divide, the left to Turquoise Lake.

Shortly beyond the fork one of the most pleasing views of the trip opens up before you. Rocky Gros Ventre Peak, frequently capped with snow through the end of July, reaches over 11,000 feet into the southwestern skyline. Two unnamed peaks each over 10,500 feet flank both sides of Gros Ventre Peak, forming an impressive stretch of peaks towering 1,000 ft. above you. The trail drops to a tributary of Granite Creek at 10.2 miles before resuming its gradual climb until, at 10.9 miles, you descend the last .1 miles to the turquoise waters that give the lake its name. There are numerous campsites in the vicinity of the lake, many frequently used by horse parties. Choose your site judiciously and be sure to treat your water.

Returning via Cache Creek is an attractive option but lacks the one advantage gained by retracing your footsteps: a long soak in the hot springs pool near the beginning of the trail. The natural hot springs was converted into a swimming pool by the CCC in the 1930s. It's average temperature is 112°, making it a popular destination for cross-country skiers and snowmobilers in the winter months. A modest fee is charged for its use.

▲

61 WEST DELL CREEK FALLS

Distance:
    7.5 miles one-way
Elevation gain:
    1,580 ft.
Elevation loss:
    140 ft.
Maximum elevation:
    8,240 ft.
Maps:
    Doubletop Peak

A waterfall and proximity to the highest peaks in the Gros Ventre make the hike to West Dell Creek Falls a favorite choice amongst nearby Bondurant residents. The hike is particularly appealing in autumn, when shimmering gold aspen leaves offer stark contrast to cobalt colored sky and

West Dell Creek Falls

white-capped peaks. By early October, most of the cattle that graze the high meadows have moved to lower ground, surrendering their buffet table to hikers, hunters and the critters they hunt. Walk safely: wear orange.

To reach the trailhead, drive south out of Jackson on U.S. Hwy. 89/191 for 13 miles to Hoback Junction. Turn left here, driving towards Pinedale on U.S. Hwy. 189/191. Set your odometer at the junction: 17.7 miles beyond it, almost directly opposite the Elkhorn Store, you'll see a wide, graveled Forest Service road on your left.

Turn in here and drive 3.6 miles to Little Jenny Ranch Headquarters. Drive past the headquarters several hundred yards to an unmarked, green Forest Service gate on the left. Turn in, go through that gate then another in quick succession, remembering to close the gates behind you. Straight ahead is an elk feeding ground. To your right is the rough, rutted jeep road up Parody Draw. High clearance, four-wheel drive vehicles can continue for a mile or so; sedans and low-clearance vehicles should park here. Mileage for the hike begins at this point.

The rough road travels northeast, gradually climbing to a creek crossing at Parody Draw at .8 miles; Rock Creek is crossed .6 miles further. At 1.8 miles, the road splits at a poorly defined junction. Turn right (E) here. The faint road follows a fence marked by a yellow Forest Service boundary sign before crossing House Creek. Although the 1967 Doubletop Peak topo shows the jeep road continuing a mile beyond this point, it no longer exists. Clearly a trail beyond House Creek, the path climbs north to skirt private property. It drops down to West Dell Creek at the three mile mark. Here, a long 10,000-11,000 foot ridge peeks through pretty aspen groves. It's northern end is capped by 11,682 foot Doubletop Peak, the highest mountain in the Gros Ventre.

At 3.8 miles, the trail cuts through a small meadow studded with house-sized boulders and enters sparse woods, crossing and recrossing West Dell Creek several times before reaching a long meadow at five miles. A mile further, it crosses the creek again and begins climbing at a moderate then steeper grade through wooded terrain before traversing open country at seven miles. Here, numerous cattle trails make you wonder if you are in the right place. Which one you are on is not critical. Continue heading north above the creek. Soon, you'll see the falls spilling down a rock face to your right. Heading towards them will bring you to an overlook. A use trail leads to their base.

▲

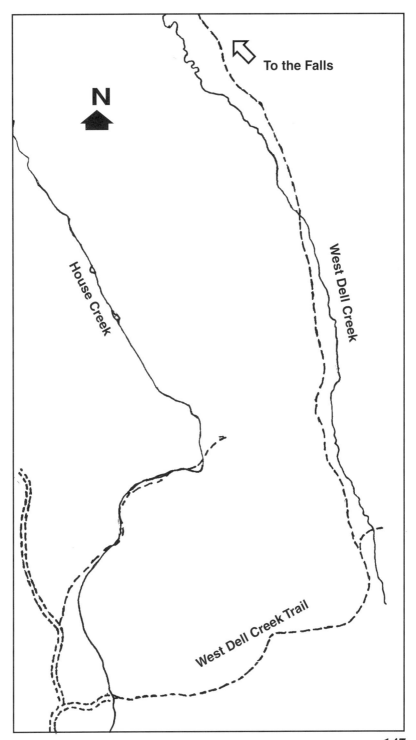

JACKSON

▲

The fashion rage of beaver top hats brought mountain men to Jackson Hole at the start of the 1800s. By mid-century, when beaver in the valley had been trapped close to extinction, fashion turned her fickle head and declared that top hats were passe. Most of the trappers left, and for almost 40 years few people outside of Indians following the game migration routes visited the valley.

Ranching and farming potential drew the first permanent homesteaders in 1884. John Holland, Mike Detweiler, John Carnes and his Indian wife, Millie, moved to the valley to farm. The next five years, the number of settlers slowly grew to 40. In the fall of 1889, the population exploded when five Mormon families crossed Teton Pass in wagons to escape the drought in Idaho and begin a new life ranching. The Wilson clan had arrived.

Overall, growth was slow, limited by the long, cold winters, marginally profitable ranching and inaccessibility. A primitive road was not built through Hoback Canyon until 1911; the first automobile wheezed over the 19% grades of Teton Pass in 1914. Two years later, the first car crested the old wagon road over Togwotee Pass. Snake River Canyon did not have road access until 1936. Even after roads were built, mountain passes were often closed from the first snows through spring thaw. As late as 1948 a local newspaper, the *Jackson Hole Courier*, reported that the valley had been completely snowbound for twelve days.

Inaccessibility limited early visitation to several groups of people: outlaws and remittance men who were seeking a place to lay low, and wealthy dudes who could afford to travel and stay at high-priced guest ranches. Only after the end of World War II—with the advent of improved automotive technology, roads, and a booming national economy—did Jackson and neighboring Grand Teton and Yellowstone National parks register significant visitation increases.

Still, with only three months of the year to make a living, the local population and range of services remained limited. Introduction in the mid-60s of a major ski area at Teton Village moved Jackson towards a two-season economy. Now, almost 30 years later, it has evolved into a year-round resort. Amenities include two ski areas, two golf courses, hundreds of condominiums and hotel units, a full-service hospital, over 70 restaurants, three live theaters, seven movie screens, and 20 plus art galleries. Fast food franchises and discount stores are de rigeur. Only a faint echo of its cow town heritage is found in the few remaining ranches, wooden boardwalks and false-front western buildings around the Town Square.

A popular destination, Jackson's primary draw remains "the Hole" in which she sits. Grand Teton National Park begins five miles north of town. The south entrance of Yellowstone is 50 miles away; vast Teton Wilderness just over 30 miles distant, and the Wind River Range 40 miles to the east. And right beyond the edge of town rise the Gros Ventres. Cache Creek Canyon begins at the end of Cache Creek Drive, a town street. Goodwin Lake and Jackson Peak are accessed by driving to the end of Broadway, then turning into the National Elk Refuge. There are few communities in the United States where you can reach three wilderness areas and two national parks in less than an hour drive, or hike from the outskirts of town.

A wealth of outdoor information is available in various vistors' centers, local bookstores, mountaineering and sporting goods stores, as well as every conceivable piece of outdoor equipment, maps, and backcountry food. For further information on the trails described in this section, please contact:

>Bridger-Teton National Forest
>Jackson Ranger District
>Box 1689
>Jackson, Wyoming 83001
>307-739-5400

62 CACHE CREEK/GAME CREEK

Distance:
    5.2 miles one-way
Elevation gain:
    730 ft.
Maximum elevation:
    7,410 ft.
Maps:
    Cache Creek

Located on the outskirts of town, Cache Creek is a popular destination for nearby or after-work forays into the backcountry. The pretty, well-maintained trail winds through wooded Cache Creek Canyon into the Gros Ventre Range. By shuttling a car or arranging a pick-up at the Game Creek Road off U.S. Hwy. 89/191 6.3 miles south of town, a pleasant 5.2 mile excursion can be completed.

From the traffic light on the town square head east on Broadway to Redmond Street, located across from St. John's Hospital. Turn right on Redmond and drive five blocks to Cache Creek Drive, which leads to the trailhead parking area roughly 2.2 miles beyond the Redmond Street turnoff.

The hike starts on the old jeep road on the left side of Cache Creek. After crossing a tributary of Salt Lick Draw, swing to the south and wind between aspen stands on the hillside to your left and small ponds near the creekbed to your right. At .6 miles you'll pass a Forest Service campsite reserved for Special Use Permitees. Bear southeast and head towards the open, grassy meadows near Gin Pole Draw at 1.4 miles. The wide, open slopes lead down to the creekbed, offering a clear view of a beaver lodge and series of dams. As you continue upwards the canyon narrows and re-enters the trees before crossing a tributary of Cache Creek at 2.5 miles. A couple of hundred yards further down the trail the summit of 10,304 foot Cache Peak pops into view, balanced on both sides by two substantial but unnamed Gros Ventre peaks. Near here a trail turn-off marked "To Game Creek" forks right and crosses Cache Creek to a double path on the other side. Follow the double path for about 15 yards, watching carefully for a sharp right-hand turn up the hillside. (The double path dead-ends in another 100 yards or so in a steep drainage).

Climbing steadily up the hillside brings you to the saddle between Game and Cache Creek, a nice turn-around point if you don't want to deal with car shuttle logistics. The hike's high point of 7,410 feet offers good views of the surrounding terrain as well as an impressive wildflower display on the grassy slopes leading to

Game Creek. To proceed out via Game Creek, drop into the basin and climb a small rise a half-mile away. From the rise descend into a dry drainage at four miles. The trail stays in this drainage and not on the ridge south of it, as indicated on the topo map. A small spring erupts near the bottom of the drainage just before it flows into Game Creek. Keep to the right where the drainage joins Game Creek. You'll pass a number of beaver ponds and lodges before reaching the Game Creek Trailhead, a total distance of 5.2 miles.

Those looking for a longer day hike should consider walking past the Game Creek turnoff to the top of Cache Creek Pass, then take the trail heading north towards Curtis Canyon and Goodwin Lake, perhaps stopping to explore the mines in Noker Mine Draw on the way up. The mines were named for John Noker, who extracted coal in Little Granite and Cache Creeks in the mid-1940s. He closed his operation when oil and electricity became the preferred heating fuels.

The hike up Cache Creek Canyon to the pass and down Curtis Canyon is roughly 12 miles. Arrange to have someone pick you up, or shuttle a car to the Goodwin Lake parking area. Directions are given in the write-up for the Goodwin Lake Hike, No. 63.

▲

63 GOODWIN LAKE & JACKSON PEAK

Distance:
    Goodwin Lake: 6 miles RT
    Jackson Peak: 9 miles RT
Elevation gained:
    Goodwin Lake: 880 ft.
    Jackson Peak: 2,380 ft.
Maximum elevation:
    Jackson Peak: 10,741 ft.
Maps:
    Cache Creek
    Turquoise Lake

Jackson Peak is one of the closest summits that can be reached from the town of Jackson. From its 10,741 foot apex, sweeping views of the Gros Ventre Range to the northeast and Jackson Hole to the west greet hikers. Goodwin Lake at its base offers fine fishing for anglers in the party, making this hike a good choice for a group with different interests.

The trailhead to Goodwin and Jackson Peak is reached by driving to the end of east Broadway and turning left into the National Elk Refuge. Follow the switchbacking dirt road as it climbs pass the turnoff to Curtis Canyon Campground at 7.5 miles to the Sheep Creek Road junction at 9.2 miles. Bear right here and drive to the trailhead parking area, a total of 10.7 miles from the National Elk Refuge entrance. The first mile of trail is a car-wide track that was formerly the last mile of road. As the path narrows, it climbs east-southeast and skirts the left of an old Forest Service clear-cut. It then crosses pine-edged open meadows colored by a kaleidoscope of wildflowers and ascends a short, steep hill. The hill tops out on a ridge shaded by limber pine. Glimpses of the lower, sheer rock walls of 10,263 ft. Sheep Mountain can be seen through occasional openings to the east.

Just before the two-mile mark the trail climbs the left side of a knoll at the end of the ridge and leaves the trees to cross a rocky clearing. Large boulders are strewn above and below the clearing, remnants of an old landslide. On the other side of the clearing the trail re-enters the woods and soon parallels the creek flowing out of Goodwin Lake. It crosses the creek at 2.8 miles, reaching the west end of the lake at three miles. Paths loop around both sides of Goodwin Lake. The wooded left (E) path leads to good campsites several hundred feet up the trail. The right fork recrosses the creek and follows the west side of the lake.

The most frequently followed approach to Jackson Peak is to stay on the trail around the left side of the lake and walk southeast for roughly one mile beyond it. As you cross open meadows and head towards an indistinct pass, the east ridge of Jackson Peak becomes obvious on your right. It is an easy but steep hike up the open slopes to the crest of the ridge, which then leads directly to the rocky summit.

A more interesting alternative is to ascend the more exposed ridge accessed from the southwest side of Goodwin Lake. This involves a steep hike up loose, rocky slopes to gain a wooded shoulder on the ridge itself before scrambling south along a narrow, rugged arete to the summit. Occasional detours on either side of the arete are required to avoid short, but difficult sections. This ascent can be combined with a descent of the "regular" east ridge to make a nice traverse of Jackson Peak.

Goodwin Lake is named after a Jackson Hole mountain man who furtrapped the numerous creeks in surrounding drainages. Goodwin would bring in a pack string of traps and supplies from Idaho before the heavy snows of November made travel difficult. After unloading and setting up a base camp, he'd send the animals home, since he had no means to feed them over the course of a long Jackson Hole winter. He trapped and lived by himself through the lonely months of December, January, February and March. Come spring, he'd cache his furs and remaining supplies and point his feet towards Idaho, eventually crossing Teton Pass to retrieve his pack string before returning to collect his hard-earned furs.

64 SNOW KING MOUNTAIN

Distance:
    1.6 miles one-way
Elevation gain:
    1,571 ft.
Maximum elevation:
    7,760 ft.
Maps:
    Jackson

The short but demanding walk up Snow King Ski Area's 7,760 foot summit will reward you with superb views of Jackson Hole. Starting with a fascinating bird's eye perspective of the town of Jackson, a longer look takes in East and West Gros Ventre Buttes and the National Elk Refuge on the valley floor, the Gros Ventre range to the northeast, and the Tetons to the northwest. Flat Creek and the Snake River meander through the unbelievably green fields of early summer in this postcard-like scene. A jaunt to the backside of the mountain reveals Leeks and Game Creek canyons, and a corner of South Park.

To reach the base of the mountain and start of the hike drive six blocks south of the Town Square on Cache Street. Park in the ballpark parking lot at the corner of Cache and Snow King Avenue. The trail is the ski area's dirt service road on the right. Please stay on the road to help minimize erosion problems on the mountain.

The first third of the walk is very steep: the altitude and the grade will immediately throw your body into its aerobic mode. Snow King is used often as an after-work "gym" by scores of locals for just this reason. The grade becomes more tolerable as the road reaches an area called Old Man Flats and enters the forested slopes higher up, finally following a series of switchbacks to top out at the saddle between Snow King's two summits. The higher, eastern summit (7,808 feet) is home to a collection of radio towers and transmitters that frequently get struck by lightning. If the weather looks suspect, you do not want to be at the base of these major lighting rods.

The top of Snow King's main chairlift crowns the 7,760 foot western summit. A half-mile nature trail lies just below. A Forest Service pamphlet is available at the obvious trailhead near the Panorama House. It describes points of interest along the short loop. In addition to an introduction to the flora and fauna of the mountain, the pamphlet mentions a tree-planting project local school chil-

The town of Jackson, seen from Snow King Mountain.

dren initiated in the early 1960s to reduce snowdrift problems in the immediate vicinity. A nice picnic area on top is the perfect spot for lunch and an outhouse is located here, as well.

There are several hiking options from the top of the mountain. The simplest is to retrace your route. Walking down the Game Creek Trail on the backside of the mountain is the longest. It requires leaving a car at the Game Creek trailhead six miles south of town beforehand or hitching a ride back to Snow King at the end of your hike. Leeks Canyon also descends the backside of the mountain. Wilson Canyon, accessed near the higher, eastern summit, involves a bushwhack down to Cache Creek on the Jackson side of Snow King. Hikers can pick up the Cache Creek Trail and by walking down to its trailhead and then along Cache Drive and Redmond Streets eventually get back to the base of Snow King. Consult appropriate maps if these routes are of interest.

Hikers who walk to the top of Snow King also have the option of a free ride down the mountain. Those interested in riding up and walking down must pay a modest lift fee. For fees and operating hours of the chairlift, call 733-5200.

The "town hill," as Snow King is known locally, is one of the oldest ski areas in the country. A rope tow began operating on the mountain in October of 1939. A lift supported by wooden towers began running to the summit of the peak in 1946. It serviced local skiers until 1981, when the current state-of-the-art lift replaced it.

155

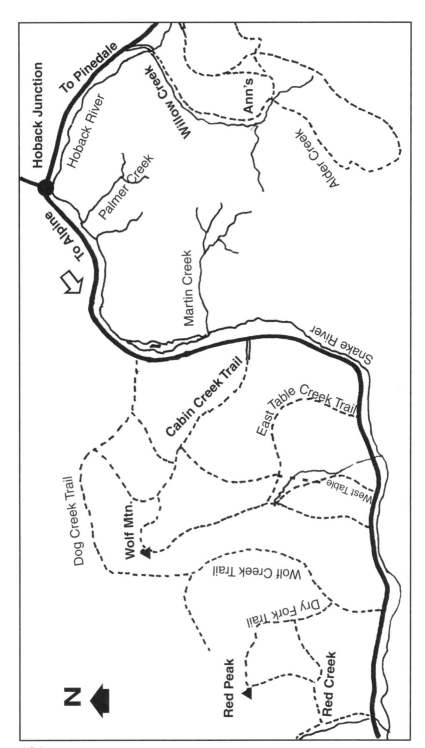

HOBACK CANYON/ SOUTH JACKSON HOLE

▲

In 1810, New Yorker John Jacob Astor started the Pacific Fur Company and immediately organized two expeditions to set up a base of operation. One went by ship through Cape Horn and entered the Columbia River, building Fort Astoria 12 miles upstream in the spring of 1811. The second expedition was an overland venture headed by William Price Hunt. His mission was to discover a route from the Missouri River to the west coast.

Hunt soon met and hired three Kentuckians heading back east to serve as guides. Edward Robinson, Jacob Reznor and John Hoback had trapped in Jackson Hole the previous year, and spoke of a route that avoided crossing territory occupied by hostile Blackfoot Indians. The trio were tough characters. Already in his 60s, Robinson had been scalped by an Indian in his home state and wore a bandana around his head to hide the scar. Wild and unruly, they apparently needed little persuasion to return to the largely unexplored country they had just left.

The Astorians were led up the Wind River then down the Green to a low pass into yet another river canyon. Hunt named the steep forested slopes and rushing river "Hoback River Canyon" in honor of his chief guide. In places the tricky route wound over 200 feet above the river, and proved difficult to negotiate. It would be another 111 years before a road was built through the canyon, providing a southeastern entrance into Jackson Hole.

After an unsuccessful attempt to reach the Pacific by floating down the Snake River, the Kentuckians led Hunt's rag-tag group of explorers and trappers out of the valley via Teton Pass (called Hunt's Pass until 1900). The group parted company near Twin Falls, Idaho. Robinson, Reznor and Hoback were all killed in 1813 when their camp on the upper tributaries of the Columbia River near Boise, Idaho, was raided by Indians.

The lower reaches of Hoback River Canyon marks the divide between the Gros Ventre Range to the north and the Wyoming Range to the south. The latter runs roughly 60 miles between the Green River to the east and Grey's River to the west. It's spine of 10,000 foot peaks includes the impressive trio of Ramshorn, Clause and Hoback peaks. The three are a beautiful backdrop for several hikes included in this section. The highest peak in the range, remote 11,380 foot Wyoming Peak, lies further south.

Named the Bear River Range when Wyoming was granted territorial status in 1868, this string of mountains was renamed in honor of statehood being achieved in 1890. Seldom visited, the attractions of the range include solitude and good opportunities to see wildlife. Trails below 9,000 feet are usually free of snow by early July; it is not uncommon for snow to remain on top of the peaks until mid-July or later.

The trails included in this section are administered by the Big Piney District. For further information, write or call:

>	Bridger-Teton National Forest
>	Big Piney Ranger District
>	Box 218
>	Big Piney, Wyoming 83113
>	307-276-3375

65 CREAM PUFF PEAK

Distance:
  9.8 miles RT
Elevation gain:
  3,485 ft.
Maximum elevation:
  9,685 ft.
Maps:
  Bull Creek

Unlike its name, the hike up 9,685 ft. Cream Puff Peak is not a cake walk. It's steadily up through hot, open hillsides on a trail that offers little relief from the sun. The same trail turns into a mud bobsled run during rainy weather. Your only hope of not sliding down the steep gradient is getting stuck in one of numerous bogs created by horses.

That warning given, I think Cream Puff is one of the nicest peak hikes on the southern end of Jackson Hole. I've often seen deer or bighorn sheep on the lower stretches. Wildflowers are prolific and varied, including not often seen wild hollyhocks, sugar bowl and sego lilies. The view from the summit is superb. North, the Tetons are displayed from Teton Pass to Mt. Moran. The Gros Ventre Range fills the eastern skyline, while the distant Winds are seen to the southeast. Continuing the panoramic circle, the Hoback, Wyoming and Salt River ranges define the southern sky. West, the Palisades and Snake River ranges are seen. I've lingered longer on this summit than many others.

To reach the trailhead, drive south of Jackson on U.S. Hwy. 189/191 13 miles to Hoback Junction. Here, stay left and drive towards Pinedale. The highway crosses three bridges over the Hoback River, the last 9.8 miles from the junction. Begin watching carefully. At 10.6 miles you'll reach the turn-off up Bull Creek on your left. Drive .1 miles up the dirt road, and park in the grassy area to your right. (Note: the trailhead has been moved since the topo was plotted. The new path joins the trail as plotted at .4 miles. Don't be confused.)

Walk a short distance up the road, looking ahead to your left at the edge of the trees. Tucked at the base of the trees you should see a Forest Service trail marker signed "Cow Creek Trail."

From the trailhead, the path travels south briefly before bending west and paralleling the highway below, gradually climbing to an intersection at .4 miles. This is the end of the former Cow Creek jeep road shown on the map. Walk straight at the intersection, continuing to ascend through open slopes sprinkled with delicate blue flax in mid-summer. Soon, you'll pass under a powerline. The pole is marked with a "National Forest Wilderness" sign, reminding users that it is closed to both motorized equipment and mountain bikes.

Continue to climb up sage and grass-covered hillsides, enjoying views of long, snow-covered Beaver Mountain to your left. Beaver's three summits are measured at 9,854 feet, 9,755 feet, and 9,635 feet.

At .8 miles, the trail briefly switchbacks and begins angling more steadily northwest away from the highway. Cow Creek is heard but unseen below you to your left. The trail drops slightly than resumes its relentless climb up the creek drainage. The trail soon divides, the first of many splits. Take either side: it always merges into one trail.

Hop a small rivulet then the upper reaches of Cow Creek at 1.3 miles and climb towards scattered groves of aspen trees. Enter a welcome, shady stretch of aspen forest .3 miles further. Soon climb above it, gaining views of the Gros Ventre range to your right (E) and bare, cone-shaped Peak 10,013 ahead (N). The distinctive monolith behind it to the right is 10,808 foot Pinnacle Peak.

The trail jumps a small stream as if climbs to 8,400 feet at 2.2 miles—2,000 feet above your start—then descends at an easy grade. You'll soon see an outfitters camp as you lose elevation. Above the camp is a long,

The hike to Cream Puff Peak yields expansive views of the surrounding Gros Ventre Range.

grassy ridge. Cream Puff is the peak at its left (SW) end.

The trail drops 200 feet in half a mile, reaching the outfitters picnic table(!) at 2.7 miles. Here, the trail seems to disappear. Look right at the two o'clock position to a clear trail up the hill. Cross a boggy meadow to reach it and resume climbing. Stay left where the trail splits, entering a lodgepole and whitebark pine forest at three miles. Here, the trail begins climbing very steeply, its path clearly marked by tree blazes. In roughly .3 miles, and a gain of over 200 feet, it forks. Take the obvious trail to the left to continue on to Cream Puff. That trail soon leaves the woods and angles at a more reasonable grade up open, grassy slopes to the end of the ridge at 4.7 miles. From here, it is an easy walk to the top of Cream Puff's summit, .2 miles further.

A second option is to walk right at the split. This steep trail leads almost due west through the woods, reaching the open slopes of the ridge between Cream Puff and an unnamed peak to the northeast at 3.8 miles. Here, the Grand Teton is seen to the distance north. The trail continues past interesting rock outcroppings as it ascends to peak 9,720, whose two summits are separated by a small saddle. Walk to the furthest for the best views of the panorama below.

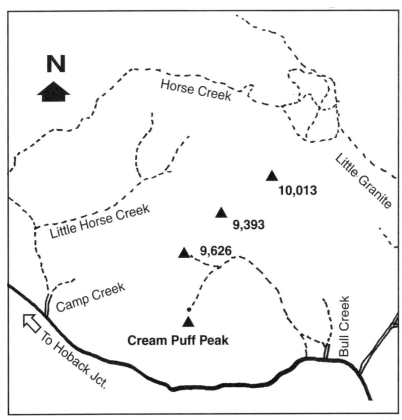

66 MONUMENT RIDGE

Distance:
 5 miles RT
Elevation gained:
 1,077 ft.
Maximum elevation:
 8,257 ft.
Maps:
 Bondurant

Monument Ridge is an early season favorite. A gentle climb through newly-budded aspens and impossibly green ridges leads to an abandoned fire lookout tower and a panoramic view of distant blue, snow-capped peaks. A 360-degree spin on top takes in the high peaks of the Wyoming, Snake River, Teton and Gros Ventre ranges. Chances of seeing antelope and moose on the way to the lookout are better than average, and delicate, dark purple Larkspur and hearty yellow "Mule's Ears" on the hillsides announce the arrival of summer.

The trailhead is reached by driving 13 miles south out of Jackson on U.S. Hwy 89/191 to Hoback Junction. Head left at the junction and drive another 22 miles to the small town of Bondurant. Roughly two miles out of town a small green, metal telephone utility shed stands at the entrance of a dirt road on the right-hand side of the highway. Turn here and drive .5 miles to a fork. Turn right again and follow the muddy, bumpy road up Clark's Draw to its end. It is not uncommon to have to park a half mile before the end of the road, where an intermittent tributary may make further car travel a dicey proposition.

At road's end the trail immediately crosses Clark Creek and heads west across sage-covered slopes, climbing 340 feet in .7 miles to the first of three switchbacks up pleasant aspen groves. At 1.2 miles, you intersect an old jeep trail. Turn hard right to access Monument Ridge (walking on the path that turns slightly right will take you out Sandy Marshall Creek). Gently climb 500 feet over the next mile or so, reaching an intersection with Little Cliff Creek pack trail on your left (W) at 2.3 miles. To your right the ridge drops off steeply to a series of small lakes at the head of Miller Draw. Continue straight another .2 miles to the crest of Monument Ridge at 8,257 feet.

The fire lookout tower is usually unlocked and offers a hospitable place to retreat if the wind is blowing. But its less-than-clean windows don't provide the view that you get outside. To the southwest and west the Wyoming Range shows off its snowy peaks, including 10,862 foot Hoback Peak; 10,612 foot Clause Peak and 10,368 foot Ramshorn Peak. To the north the high summits of the Gros Ventre dominate. To the south the rim of Hoback Canyon is defined. With a green foreground and ragged, snow-covered peaks as a backdrop, the scene looks like the opening shot in "The Sound of Music."

Those desiring a longer hike can access the ridge by walking up the trail from the signed Hoback Guard Station, 1.1 miles before the town of Bondurant. The four mile trail gains an additional 600 feet in elevation.

▲

67 ANN'S RIDGE
68 WILLOW CREEK

Distance:
    Ann's Ridge: 1.6 miles one-way
    Willow Creek loop: 6.2 miles
Elevation gain:
    Ann's Ridge: 1,111 ft.
    Willow Creek loop: 1,111 ft.
Elevation loss:
    Willow Creek loop: 910 ft.
Maximum elevation:
    7,444 ft.
Maps:
    Camp Davis

The hike to Ann's Ridge and the longer Willow Creek loop hike beyond it shed their snow early, and neither are difficult in terms of ascent or distance. Both factors happily combine to make them a good first hike of the season. While the scenery lacks the breathtaking property of the high country, the hikes are pleasant and offer a good opportunity to see moose and deer. A short car shuttle is necessary to complete the loop hike. Without a shuttle, add three miles of road walking to the total mileage.

To reach the trailhead, drive 13 miles south of Jackson on U.S. Hwy. 89/191 to Hoback Junction. At the junction, turn left towards Pinedale on U.S. Hwy. 189/191 and drive 4.4 miles to an unmarked dirt road on your right. Turn in here. At .4 miles, the road crosses a bridge over the Hoback River. Shortly after the bridge, a private road to the right leads to Camp Davis. Continue straight, driving past a dirt road at one mile that

The view from Ann's Ridge of Peak 7,450.

leads to private residences to the right, the Hoback River to the left. At 1.5 miles, you'll reach the signed Willow Creek Trailhead parking area on your right.

The trail switchbacks uphill a short distance then follows fenced property to a gate. After passing through the gate it turns left and follows the fence line uphill through sparse aspen forest. This area has been significantly cut by the Forest Service to stimulate growth of the young understory and improve wildlife habitat in the area.

Stay to the left where the trail splits and jump over a small unnamed creek. The trail continues pass a second gate to your left has it proceeds south. It curves right (W) away from the fence at .4 miles, just before reaching another fence gate with a prominent No Trespassing sign. (Pay attention here, as a fainter use trail continues straight.)

The trail climbs through light lodgepole forest and small clearings, home to huckleberry bushes, before reaching a small pond at .6 miles. Don't be surprised if you see cattle: this is grazing country. Don't be surprised if you also see moose, which abound in the area.

From the pond, the trail ascends at a moderate, steady grade through heavier forest to the ridge crest at 1.2 miles. An old sign, already on the ground and probably doomed for extinction, reads "Bryan Flats Guard Station - 1." A newer sign, still standing, directs you left to Lick and Upper Willow Creeks, or straight to Alder Creek, reached in one mile.

To reach Ann's Ridge:
Follow the obvious use trail to your right at the junction. The trail takes

you up a wide, sage and grass-covered ridge. There is no obvious high point. The use trail, not plotted on the 1965 Camp Davis topo, continues west. Follow it, dropping slightly, to a large grassy area that provides a view of the Tetons from Teton Pass to the Grand. The dominant peak to your right (E), seen at numerous spots on the way up, is Peak 7,450. The use trail here continues down to Lafayette Guard Station near Camp Davis, not a viable option since you must cut through private property to get to your car. Return the way you came, or loop back to the highway via the Willow Creek Trail.

To do the Willow Creek loop:
At the junction, continue straight (SW) towards Alder Creek, reached in one mile. Instead of crossing the footbridge over that creek, take the trail to your right (W). The path leads west for .5 miles, then swings north and gently descends the Willow Creek drainage, crossing the creek at 3 and 3.5 miles. Sourdough Creek is crossed at the 5 mile mark. A mile further, the well-signed trail departs from the plotted course on the topo map. Because private property owners do not want hikers crossing their land to reach a footbridge over the Hoback River, the trail presently turns right (SE) and follows the Forest Service easement to a float trip and camping concession operated by Lone Eagle. Stop in, buy a coke and a snack, and thank the people operating the business for not restricting recreational access to public land. If you do a shuttle in advance, ask them where it would be good for you to park so you don't negatively impact their business operations. The turn-off to Lone Eagle is 3.9 miles beyond Hoback Junction, .5 miles before the dirt turn-off that leads to the Willow Creek Trailhead.

▲

69 CLIFF CREEK FALLS

Distance:
 12.4 miles RT
Elevation gain:
 1,100 ft.
Maximum elevation:
 8,040 ft.
Maps:
 Hoback Peak
 Clause Peak

Beautiful Cliff Creek Falls is a favorite destination of Bondurant residents and a handful of Jacksonites who've heard about it through friends. The trail passes through varied terrain on its way to the falls, a two-tiered silver spray that drops first down a short upper falls before plunging another 50 feet or so to the bottom of Cliff Creek. Enroute to the falls you'll walk past striking red bands of granite, forested slopes, hillsides denuded by avalanches, basins of willows and conifers, and sunny, open meadows filled with the reds, violets and yellows of wildflowers from early June through mid-August.

Drive south out of Jackson on U.S. Highway 89/191 for 13 miles to Hoback Junction. There, stay left to access U.S. Highway 189/191 towards Pinedale, a pretty route that takes you into the heart of Hoback Canyon. Pass the turnoff to Granite Falls Recreation Area 11.8 miles further and drive another 3.4 miles to the signed junction with Cliff Creek Road on the right-hand side of the highway. Follow the well-maintained dirt road 7.1 miles to the trailhead and park alongside the road.

Take out your sneakers and prepare to wade fast, ice-cold Cliff Creek just below the confluence with Sandy Marshall Creek. If you have a four-wheel drive vehicle with high clearance it is possible to drive across the creek and follow jeep tracks south for a half mile, where the trail turns into a dirt lane climbing west through conifers. The path ascends a sage-covered rise before dropping into a small drainage and following gently rolling terrain studded with patches of trees. At the one mile mark it skirts the base of a talus field. Stay right where an unmarked spur trail veers to the left, walking by large pines to the Snag Creek Junction at 1.4 miles. Continue southwest up the valley, cross a tributary of Cliff Creek at 1.6 miles, and gradually climb through a pleasant forest of spruce and fir trees before walking around a rise and crossing two braids of Cabin Creek at 2.3 miles. Walk past the junction to Ramshead Trail shortly beyond the creek and ascend a small hill to the junction with Bondurant Creek and Honeymoon Lake Trail at 2.6 miles. The Cliff Creek Trail continues its southwesterly direction as it passes alternately through open hillsides colored with wildlflowers and groves of aspen and conifers, then passes below red talus slopes at 3.5 miles.

You'll cross and recross Cliff Creek before reaching several ponds roughly five miles from the trailhead, then pass hillsides eroded by tributaries tumbling down their slopes. Conifers and aspens are replaced by stately cottonwood trees that thrive in the wetter environment.

Two tributaries join in a lush meadow at 5.5 miles. At its end the trail winds through the first of numerous avalanche paths before contouring up a steeper section of the secluded valley, reaching the head of Cliff Creek Canyon just past the six-mile mark. Cliff Creek Falls cuts through the western end of the box canyon bounded by 10,579 foot Clause Peak to the north and 10,864 foot Hoback Peak to the south. The fine spray from the falls often catches the sun and paints a rainbow near the bottom.

Although not shown of the topo maps, a faint trail can be found on the hillside west of the falls. This leads south towards Cliff Creek Pass and Hoback Canyon, offering the possibility of a fine two or three day backpacking trip in the Wyoming Range.

70 MUNGER MOUNTAIN

Distance:
    2.6 miles one-way
Elevation gain:
    2,140 feet
Maximum elevation:
    8,383 feet
Maps:
    Munger Mountain

Munger Mountain was the site of one of six fire lookout stations constructed in the northern portion of Teton National Forest by the Civilian Conservation Corps (CCC's) in the 1930s. It was chosen for clear, unobstructed views of the Teton Range to the north, Snake River Range to the west, the Wyoming Range to the south and the Gros Ventres to the east.

The lookout and incredible wildflowers enroute enticed hikers through the late 1950s, when the Forest Service stopped using the structure. New fire policies, reporting done by public and private aircraft, and use of radio repeaters had doomed fire towers to extinction. Some hikers and skiers continued to visit the lookout—often staying overnight—until the Forest Service burnt the structure down in 1976. According to Forest Service archeologist Jamie Schoen, the towers at Deer Creek, Baldy Mountain and Munger were considered fire hazards! Towers at Signal Mountain and Blacktail Butte were dismantled by the National Park Service in 1943. Only Huckleberry Lookout remains (see hike no. 51).

The pack trail to the razed lookout was abandoned and gradually fell out of use. It is not difficult to access the summit, however, and it is worth the walk up. To avoid looking like you've been attacked by crazed cats, consider wearing long pants on this cross-country jaunt through sage and other prickly things.

To reach the trailhead, drive south of Jackson on U.S. Hwy. 89/191 for 13 miles to Hoback Junction. Here, turn right towards Alpine on U.S. Hwy. 26/89. Drive 4.3 miles to the signed Wilson-Fall Creek Road turn-off on your right. Turn unto this road and drive 3.2 miles to a bridge over Fall Creek. Just beyond the bridge, turn right unto a narrow dirt road. (Alternately, you may reach this point by driving south down Fall Creek Road 13.8 miles from its start off Wyoming Hwy. 22 in Wilson). Cross the cattle guard and find a place to park. Two-tenths of a mile further, a dirt two-track heads left (N). Follow this to its end; it narrows into the former trail.

The path clearly climbs then contours around a hill before disappearing into a jungle of waist-high flowers. Don't waist your time looking for a trail. Walk uphill, staying to the right of the creek. When the grade noticeably flattens, hop the creek and pick up a game/cattle trail that leads left (W) to a flat, denuded piece of ground where there is often a salt block. Here, it is easy to pick out a trail up the hill to your right. Follow it until it, too, peters out. Continue to ascend the sage-covered slopes, bearing slightly left. When you access the ridge, you'll pick up a clear trail again. If you miss it, walk right (SE) once you are on the ridge, ascending to its highest point.

The remains of the lookout are marked by a concrete foundation, a few rusted can lids, and a metal survey marker placed by the U.S. Coast and Geodetic Survey in 1946.

Munger Mountain was named for a prospector who mined gold at the foot of the peak, probably on its north side.

▲

71 WOLF MOUNTAIN

Distance:
    Saddle: 5.9 miles one-way
    Wolf summit: 7 miles one-way
Elevation gain:
    Saddle: 3,200 ft.
    Wolf summit: 3,900 ft.
Maximum elevation:
    Saddle: 9,200 ft.
    Wolf summit: 9,481 ft.
Maps:
    Munger Mtn.

Grassy meadows, lush wildflower-covered slopes, a rocky summit and sweeping views of the Snake River Range, Gros Ventres and the Hobacks are all components of the ambitious hike to Wolf Mountain. The distinctive peak can be reached by a number of lightly-used Forest Service trails. The description below is the trail/route up Cabin Creek.

Drive south of Jackson on U.S. Hwy. 89/191 for 13 miles to Hoback Junction. Here, drive right towards Alpine on U.S. Hwy 26/89. Set your odometer: 7.3 miles from the junction is an abrupt turn-off to a small dirt road on the right marked by a Forest Service sign that reads "Cabin Creek." Turn unto this narrow, rutted road and drive .3 miles to its end. If you are in a low-clearance vehicle, try to park at an obvious wide spot to the left of the

Hikers angle up open slopes towards Wolf Mountain's summit.

road shortly after you turn in.

At the end of the road, the trail climbs to the right, quickly ascending above Cabin Creek and horse corrals used by a fall hunting camp. The path is lined with serviceberry bushes, heavy with fruit in early autumn. It soon drops to the creek, leading you through tall grasses and scrub willow before climbing through meadow then open sagebrush slopes.

Cross a log bridge over a tributary of the creek, dry by fall, at 1.6 and again at 2.5 miles. Here, the valley begins to narrow as the trail continues its ascent.

Reach a signed junction at 3.1 miles. To reach Dog Creek, go right. Take the left fork to reach Wolf Mountain. A second signed junction, not plotted on the 1963 Munger Mountain map, is reached at 3.8 miles. The trail to the left leads to Hwy. 26, exiting at West Table Creek, in six miles. Stay right at this junction.

The trail to Wolf cuts through trees then open slopes, where it becomes increasingly sketchy but followable. Cross a tributary of the creek and enter a stand of pine and fir. Here the path seems to disappear in a carpet of pine needles. Look towards the one o'clock position and you'll see a large blaze 30 yards ahead. Walk towards the blaze, climbing over and around downed trees as you keep the stream to your right. In a short distance, you'll reach clear trail again.

Near the head of the tributary, the trail again seems to vanish in open slopes near a large, uprooted tree stump. If you gradually angle right, you'll pick it up in a half mile or less. However, sections of the upper "official" trail are washed out; other stretches have an uncomfortable slope that requires tedious side-stepping.

A recommended alternative is to proceed straight (W) from the stump. In approximately 50 yards, you'll see a wide dirt patch leading up a hillside to your left. Walk up the short, steep hill and gain a use trail that ascends a draw. Stay left where the trail splits and climb to a forested ridge. The trail contours in-and-out of the woods, providing views of the Tetons and Snake River Range. At approximately three quarters of a mile, it crosses open slopes south of Wolf Mountain and travels through a large gravel slide, reached 5 miles from the trailhead.

Leave the use trail here, and begin angling left (S) up the slope. You'll soon intersect the trail heading up from East Table Creek. Turn right unto this trail; it leads to a small saddle between Peak 9,301 to your left and Wolf Mountain to your right. The saddle is reached at 5.9 miles. It's marked by a lonely-looking wood Forest Service sign that reads "trail."

Walking right up the small knoll above the saddle is a worthy end destination. The all-encompassing view takes in the Hoback River, Snake River Range, Cabin Creek drainage, the southern end of the Tetons, and the rocky SE flank of Wolf Mountain.

To ascend that peak, drop right off the knoll to the East Table Trail and walk north for .5 miles to its intersection with the upper reaches of Cabin Creek Trail. Turn left at the junction and walk west for .2 miles until the peak is clearly visible to your left. Here it is possible to scramble up Wolf's north ridge to the summit. The view is not much different than that from the knoll.

72 RED CREEK

Distance:
 4 miles one-way
Elevation gain:
 2,650 ft.
Maximum elevation:
 8,450 ft.
Maps:
 Ferry Peak

Anyone who has floated down Snake River Canyon has gazed up at fluted, snow-covered Ferry Peak rising without preamble above the river to the west. This impressive ridge, Deadhorse and Red peaks command the skyline on the hike up lightly-visited Red Creek north of the Snake River Canyon. Striking rock cliffs, flowered meadows, high-country views and an overlook of Dry Fork Canyon are featured on this hike.

To reach the trailhead, drive 13 miles south of Jackson on U.S. Hwy. 89/191 to Hoback Junction. Here, turn right on U.S. Hwy. 26/87 towards Alpine. Set your odometer: 17.6 miles beyond the junction, immediately before a road sign that reads "Alpine 5, Afton 38, is the quick turn-off to Red Creek on your right.

Turn in and park. Follow the two-track north through aspen groves. At .1 miles, a faint trail to your left climbs west. This sketchy, oft-times non-existent trail leads to Deadhorse Peak. Stay right and cross Red Creek at .2 miles. The trail heads north as it skirts the base of rock cliffs to your right (E). It follows the creek as it ascends the canyon, crossing it again at 1.1 miles. Here, it bends right (E) and climbs more steeply up an open draw for .9 miles. At two miles, it switchbacks left (W) to the top of the draw. A trail to an abandoned herder's camp, marked by point 7,525 on the topo leads to the left. Stay right. The trail forms a semi-circle as it turns northeast then south on its contour up and around a hillside on good trail.

At 3.1 miles, the trail intersects the route down Blind Canyon, marked by a rock cairn. It is here that the trail on the ground begins to diverge from the topo map. Where the map shows a path leading north towards Red Peak, the trail heads right (E) at approximately 8,400 feet, contours above Open Canyon, and ends at a small saddle overlooking Dry Fork Canyon, east of point 8,536 on the topo. This is a nice end destination to a pretty hike. Those wishing to loop hike up to Red Peak and walk west to Deadhorse Peak, then back to their vehicle via Little Red Creek, should bring a compass to help plot their route. The trails shown on the map are not clearly visible on the ground.

The view looking north towards Red Peak.

73 ELK MOUNTAIN

Distance:
   3 miles one-way
Elevation gain:
   2,300 ft.
Maximum elevation:
   8,513 ft.
Maps:
   Pine Creek

In the 1930s, Forest Service officials established 12 permanent lookout stations on the Bridger-Teton National Forest to aid in fire detection. The towers were built using CCC labor. Most were constructed of log at low elevations, taken apart and marked, then re-assembled at their respective mountain top or ridge.

One of the lookout stations was on top of 8,513 foot Elk Mountain. The site was chosen because of clear views north of the Snake River and Teton ranges, south of the ridges and peaks of the Salt River Range and the Middle Ridge. The vantage point makes it a great hiking destination, as does its comparative solitude. That summer rarity is created by the hike's distance from Grand Teton and Yellowstone park traffic.

To reach the trailhead, drive south of Jackson 13 miles on U.S. Hwy. 189/191 to Hoback Junction. Stay right here, traveling south 29 miles on U.S. 26/89 through winding Snake River Canyon to Alpine Junction. Turn left at the junction, cross a bridge over Palisades Reservoir, and almost immediately turn left unto the signed Greys River Road. 8.3 miles down this well-maintained gravel road, turn left again at the signed Little Greys River intersection. Proceed east for 1.2 miles to a marked turn-off to your left that reads: "Trail Creek and Pine Creek Trails. Elk Mountain 3, Snake River 7." Drive a short distance up this rough dirt road and park.

The obvious trail leads northeast through scattered forest and open areas, paralleling Trail Creek as it ascends at a steady, moderately steep grade. There are numerous game/hunter use trails in the area not shown on the topo. At the first trail split, stay right; at the second, go left. Pass an interesting rocky area to your left at 1.5 miles.

The trail climbs to the south above it. At two miles, you reach an obvious dip in a ridge that opens up views of the Teton Range. Go right here. In three-quarters mile, the trail turns sharply northwest. Ahead of you is the small lookout, reached in 15-20 more minutes.

BIBLIOGRAPHY

▲

Allan, Esther. *History of Teton National Forest.* Unpublished, 1973.
Betts, Robert A. *Along the Ramparts of the Tetons: The Saga of Jackson Hole.* Boulder, Colorado: Colorado Associated University Press, 1978.
Bonney, Orrin and Lorraine. *Guide to the Wyoming Mountains and Wilderness Areas, Third Edition.* Chicago, Illinois: Sage Press, 1977.
Burt, Nathaniel. *Jackson Hole Journal.* Norman, Oklahoma: University of Oklahoma Press, 1983.
Burt, William Henry. *A Field Guide to the Mammals.* Boston,

Massachusetts: Houghton Mifflin Company, 1964.
Calkins, Frank. *Jackson Hole.* New York, New York: Alfred A. Knopf, 1973.
Carter, Tom. *Day Hiking in Grand Teton National Park.* Garland, Texas: Dayhiking Press, 1993.
Fryxell, Fritiof. *Mountaineering in the Tetons: The Pioneer Period 1898-1940.* Jackson, Wyoming: Teton Bookshop.
Hayden, Elizabeth Wied. *From Trappers to Tourists in Jackson Hole.* Moose, Wyoming: Grand Teton Natural History Association, 1981.
Hunger, Bill. *The Hiker's Guide to Wyoming.* Billings, Montana: Falcon Press, 1992.
Jackson, Reynold and Ortenburger, Leigh. *A Complete Climber's Guide to the Teton Range, Draft Edition.* Self-published, 1990.
Larson, T.A. *Wyoming: A History.* New York, New York: W.W. Norton & Company, 1984.
Lawrence, Paul. *Hiking the Teton Backcountry.* San Francisco, California: Sierra Club Books, 1973.
Maughan, Ralph. *Beyond the Tetons.* Boulder, Colorado: Pruett Publishing, 1981.
Nielsen, Cynthia & Hayden, Elizabeth Wied. *Origins: A Guide to the Place Names of Grand Teton NationalPark and the Surrounding Area.* Moose, Wyoming: Grand Teton Natural History Association, 1988.
Perry, Jane and John. *The Sierra Club Guide to the Natural Areas of Idaho, Montana and Wyoming.* San Francisco, California: Sierra Club Books, 1988.
Pitcher, Don. *Wyoming Handbook, Second Edition.* Chico, California: Moon Publications, 1993.
Platts, Doris B. *The Pass: Historic Teton Pass and Wilson, Wyoming.* Wilson, Wyoming: Self-published, 1988.
Platts, Doris B. *Wilson, Wyoming Hoorah!* Wilson,Wyoming: Self-published, 1995.
Saylor, David J. *Jackson Hole, Wyoming: In the Shadow of the Tetons.* Norman, Oklahoma: University of Oklahoma Press, 1977.
Shaw, Richard. *Plants of Yellowstone and Grand Teton National Parks.* Salt Lake City, Utah: Wheelwright Press, 1974.
Urbanek, Mae. *Wyoming Place Names.* Missoula, Montana: Mountain Press Publishing Company, 1988.

APPENDIX

▲

GRAND TETON NATIONAL PARK

PHONE NUMBERS
Emergency .... 911 or Park Dispatch at 739-3301.
Visitor Information 739-3600
Weather 739-3611
Backcountry & river information (recorded) 739-3602
Campground Information (recorded) 739-3603
Climbing Information 739-3604
TDD (Telecommunications for the Deaf) 739-3400

MAILING ADDRESS
Grand Teton National Park & John D. Rockefeller, Jr., Memorial Parkway, P.O. Drawer 170, Moose, Wyoming, 83012-0170.

INFORMATION/VISITOR CENTERS
Moose Visitor Center
Located at Moose, .5 miles west of Moose Junction on the Teton Park Road. Open daily 8 a.m. to 5 p.m. through May 13 and after September 4; extended summer service is from 8 a.m. to 6 p.m. May 14—June 3, and 8 a.m. to 7 p.m. June 4—September 4. Phone 307-739-3399. Telecommunications service for the deaf (TDD): 307-739-3400.
Colter Bay Visitor Center
Located .5 miles west of Colter Bay Junction on Highway 89/191/287. Open daily 8 a.m. to 5 p.m. May 13—May 21; extended summer service is from 8 a.m. to 7 p.m. May 14—June 3, and 8 a.m. to 8 p.m. June 4—September 4. Fall hours are 8 a.m. to 5 p.m. September 5—October 1. Phone 307-739-3594.
Jenny Lake Visitor Center
Located 8 miles north of Moose Junction on the Inner Park Road. Open daily 8 a.m. to 7 p.m. June 4—September 4.
Flag Ranch Information Station
Located at Flagg Ranch, 15 miles north of Colter Bay on Highway 89/191/287. Open daily 9 a.m. to 6 p.m. June 4—September 4.

MEDICAL SERVICE
Grand Teton Medical Clinic
Located near Chevron Station at Jackson Lake Lodge. Open daily 10 a.m. to 6 p.m. late May through mid-October. Call 307-543-2514.
Hospital
St. John's Hospital in Jackson, Wyoming. Call 307-733-3636.

CAMPING
Grand Teton National Park operates five campgrounds. As of the summer of 1996, the fee is $10 per site per night. Jenny Lake Campground is open to tents only. Other campgrounds service tents, RVs and trailers. Maximum length of stay is seven days at popular Jenny Lake, 14 days at other park locations. All campgrounds operate on a first-come, first-serve basis: advance reservations are not accepted. Most of the sites fill daily during July and August, some as early as 8 a.m. For status of the different sites, ask at the entrances or visitor centers. Camping is not permitted along roadsides, at overlooks or in parking areas, nor is having more than one party at a site.

Campgrounds	Open/Close	Fill Time
GROS VENTRE 360 sites, trailer dumping station	Late April/Early Oct.	Evening
JENNY LAKE 49 sites, tents only	Late May/Late Sept.	8 a.m.
SIGNAL MTN. 86 sites, trailer dumping station	Early May/Mid-Oct.	10 a.m.
COLTER BAY 310 sites, showers, laundry, trailer dumping station, propane available	Late May/Late Sept.	Noon
LIZARD CREEK 60 sites	Early June/Early Sept.	2 p.m.

Group Camping
There are 15 group sites in the park, 10 at Colter Bay and five at the Gros Ventre Campground. Site capacities range from 10 to 75 people. The nightly fee is $2 per person. Advance reservations are required. Reservations can be secured by writing: Permits Office, Grand Teton National Park, Moose, Wyoming, 83012, between January 1 and May 15. The remainder of the year, stop at the visitor center at Colter Bay or park headquarters at Moose to make arrangements. Groups that use the sites are typically youth, religious or educational organizations.

FISHING
Fishing in the park conforms with Wyoming and National Park Service regulations, available at the Moose, Jenny Lake and Colter Bay visitor centers. A Wyoming fishing license is required to fishing the park and the parkway. Licenses may be purchased at the Moose Village Store, Signal Mountain Lodge, Colter Bay Marina and Flagg Ranch Village.

BACKPACKING
Backpackers are required to obtain a free permit for overnight trips at the Moose Visitor Center, Colter Bay Visitor Center or Jenny Lake Ranger Station. Camping is allowed in the backcountry in specific sites, or in zones. Pets are not allowed on the trails.

CLIMBING
Registration is no longer required for day climbs and off-trail hiking. The park does not check to see you are safely out of the backcountry. Make sure you leave your agenda with friends or family, so they may notify the park if you have not returned. A backcountry permit is required for overnight climbs. Obtain one at the Jenny Lake Ranger Station.

BIKING
Bicycles can only be ridden where cars can legally travel. Ride on the right side of the road in single file. **Mountain bikes or other wheeled vehicles are not permitted in the backcountry, on or off trails.**

PETS
Pets must be on a leash at all times. They are not permitted on trails or in the backcountry. Nor are they allowed in boats on the Snake River, in boats on lakes other than Jackson, or in visitor centers.

TETON WEATHER
May and June
Characterized by mild days and cool nights. Rain and occasional snow common. Depending on snowpack, the snow level stays just above the valley floor until mid-June.
July and August
Warm days and cool nights prevail, with afternoon thundershowers common. Snow level gradually retreats; high passes between canyons typically free of snow by August.
September
Sunny days and cold nights alternate with rain and occasional snowstorms. This is a wonderful time to visit the park.

Average Temp./Precipitation	May	June	July	Aug.	Sept.
Avg. High (F)	61	71	81	79	69
Avg. Low (F)	31	37	41	39	32
Avg. Snowfall (inches)	3	0	0	0	1
Avg. Rainfall (inches)	3	2	1	1	1
Avg. No. Clear Days	12	15	19	18	16

GTNP COMMERCIALLY GUIDED ACTIVITIES

The National Park Service has granted concessions to the following companies operating in Grand Teton National Park:

MOUNTAINEERING
Jackson Hole Mountain Guides & Climbing School
Provides guide service for individuals and small groups. All peaks and routes in the Teton Range. The guide service operates year-round. Classes on rock, ice and snow climbing for all ability levels. AMGA accredited. Office is in downtown Jackson. Call or write Box 7477, Jackson, Wyoming, 83001. 307-733-4979.

Exum Mountain Guides & School of American Mountaineering
The school is located at Jenny Lake. Offers daily basic and intermediate school in the park. Guides ascents of the Grand Teton. All peaks and routes. AMGA accredited. Call 733-2297 or write Box 56, Moose, Wyoming, 83012.

Climbers Ranch
Inexpensive dormitory accommodations, cooking area and showers for climbers. Sponsored by the American Alpine Club. Call 733-7271.

SNAKE RIVER FLOAT TRIPS

Most companies operate between mid-May and mid-September, depending on river flow and weather conditions. All trips are interpretive.

Barker-Ewing Float Trips—10-mile scenic trips, including morning and late evening wildlife trips. Departures throughout the day. Box 100, Moose, Wyoming, 83012. 307-733-1800 or 1-800-365-1800.

Flagg Ranch Float Trips—Whitewater and scenic wildlife trips. Only company operating north of Jackson Lake. Whitewater trips depart every two hours starting at 10 a.m.; scenic trips twice daily. 307-543-2861. June 1 - Labor Day.

Fort Jackson Float Trips—Scenic rafting trips. Sunrise trips, guided fishing trips. 307-2583 or 1-800-735-8430.

Grand Teton Lodge Company—10-mile scenic trips, morning and afternoon departures. Picnic lunch and dinner trips, guided fishing trips. Box 240, Moran, Wyoming, 83013. 307-543-2811.

Heart Six Ranch Float Trips—10-mile scenic trips, sunrise wildlife with or without breakfast on the river. Box 70, Moran, Wyoming, 83013. 307-543-2477.

Jack Dennis Fishing Trips—Guided fishing float trips; fly or spin fishing. Lunch and instruction included. Box 3369, Jackson, Wyoming, 83001. 307-733-3270.

National Park Float Trips—10-mile scenic wildlife trips, departing throughout day. Group arrangements possible. Call 307-733-6445 or 307-733-5500.

Rivermeadows—Guided fishing trips, fly fishing only. Box 347, Wilson, Wyoming, 83014. 307-733-3674.

Signal Mountain Lodge—10-mile scenic trips, guided fishing trips. Box 50, Moran, Wyoming, 83013. 307-543-2831.

Solitude Float Trips—Five and 10-mile scenic trips. Guided fishing trips. Box 112, Moose, Wyoming, 83012. 307-733-2871.

HORSEBACK RIDING

The National Park Service has granted concessions to the following companies in Grand Teton National Park:

Colter Bay Village Corral—Breakfast and dinner rides, wagon seats available. Trail rides of various lengths. 307-543-2811.

Jackson Lake Lodge Corral—Breakfast and dinner rides, wagon seats available. 307-543-2811.

GTNP EDUCATIONAL OPPORTUNITIES

RANGER-LED ACTIVITIES
National Park Service Rangers conduct a number of free, fascinating programs on the park. Topics range from wildflower talks to lives of the early pioneers to the role of fire. A complete listing of times and programs is printed in the park newspaper, *The Teewinot*, available at park visitor centers.

TETON SCIENCE SCHOOL
Located in Grand Teton National Park, Teton Science School was once a dude ranch. The school has operated since 1967, offering natural history seminars and science education for students from third grade to adults. Academic credit is available for many courses. Topics include outdoor photography, animal tracks, archaeology, edible and medicinal plants, wildflowers, geology, and many others. For information and a free catalog, write Teton Science School, Box 68, Kelly, Wyoming, 83011, or call 307-733-4765.

GRAND TETON NATURAL HISTORY ASSOCIATION
GTNHA operates bookstores in visitor centers in Grand Teton National Park, Rockefeller Parkway, Bridger-Teton and Targhee National Forests and the National Elk Refuge. Profit from the association supports educational and interpretive programs. A mail order catalog may be obtained by writing: Grand Teton Natural History Association, P.O. Box 170, Moose, Wyoming, 83012, or calling 307-739-3403.

GTNP PEAK INDEX

By elevation order:
1. Grand Teton 13,770
2. Mount Owen 12,928
3. Middle Teton 12,804
4. Mount Moran 12,605
5. South Teton 12,514
6. Teewinot 12,325
7. Teepe's Pillar 12,266
8. Thor Peak 12,050
9. Cloudveil Dome 12,026

10. Buck Mountain 11,938
11. Nez Perce 11,901
12. Crooked Thumb 11,680
13. Disappointment Peak 11,618
14. Mount Woodring 11,590
15. Mount Wister 11,490
16. Mount St. John 11,430
17. Doane Peak 11,430
18. Ranger Peak 11,355
19. Veiled Peak 11,330
20. Eagles Rest 11,258
21. Prospectors Mountain 11,241
22. Rockchuck Peak 10,927
23. Table Mountain 11,106
24. Traverse Peak 11,051
25. McClintock Peak 11,012
26. Rendezvous Peak 10,927
27. Fossil Mountain 10,916
28. Rolling Thunder 10,908
29. Rock of Ages 10,895
30. Bivouac Peak 10,825
31. Mount Hunt 10,783
32. Ayres' Crags 10,750
33. Shadow Peak 10,725
34. Symmetry Spire 10,560
35. Storm Point 10,054

By Alphabetical Order
Ayres Crags (32) 10,750
Buck Mountain (10) 11,938
Cloudveil Dome (9) 12,026
Crooked Thumb (12) 11,680
Disappointment Peak (13) 11,618
Doane Peak (17) 11,355
Eagles Rest (20) 11,258
Fossil Mountain (27) 10,916
Grand Teton (1) 13,770
McClintock Peak (25) 11,012
Middle Teton (3) 12,804
Mount Hunt (31) 10,783
Mount Moran (4) 12,605

Mount Owen (2)	12,928
Mount St. John (16)	11,430
Mount Wister (15)	11,490
Mount Woodring (14)	11,590
Nez Perce (11)	11,901
Prospectors Mountain (21)	11,241
Ranger Peak (18)	11,355
Rendezvous Peak (26)	10,927
Rock of Ages (29)	10,895
Rockchuck Peak (22)	11,144
Rolling Thunder (28)	10,908
Shadow Peak (33)	10,725
South Teton (5)	12,514
Symmetry Spire (34)	10,560
Storm Point (35)	10,054
Table Mountain (23)	11,106
Teepe's Pillar (7)	12,266
Teewinot (6)	12,325
Thor Peak (8)	12,028
Traverse Peak (24)	11,051
Veiled Peak (19)	11,330

BRIDGER-TETON NATIONAL FOREST

PHONE NUMBERS

Emergencies	911
Fire Dispatch	307-739-5580
Avalanche Information	307-733-2664
Road Report/Conditions	1-800-442-7850
Wyoming Highway Patrol	1-800-442-9090

DISTRICT RANGER OFFICES

Kemmerer Ranger District 307-877-4415
Hwy. 189
P.O. Box 31
Kemmerer, Wyoming 83101

Big Piney Ranger District 307-276-3375
Highway 189
P.O. Box 218
Big Piney, Wyoming 83113

Greys River Ranger District 307-886-3166
125 Washington
P.O. Box 338
Afton, Wyoming 83110
Jackson Ranger District 307-739-5400
140 E. Broadway
P.O. Box 1689
Jackson, Wyoming 83001
Buffalo Ranger District 307-543-2386
Highway 287
P.O. Box 278
Moran, Wyoming 83013
Pinedale Ranger District 307-367-4326
210 W. Pine Street P.O. Box 220
Pinedale, Wyoming 82941

CAMPING

All campgrounds are on a first-come, first serve basis. Fees are based on facilities provided. Most undeveloped areas within the Forest are open to camping at no charge. Limits of stay are posted at each campground. None of the campgrounds have showers or hookups. Those listed below are on the Jackson and Buffalo districts.

Turpin Meadow
Located off Turpin Meadow/Buffalo Valley Road, accessed off Highway 287 between Moran Junction and Dubois. Open camping. Picnic tables, restrooms, drinking water, stock loading and corrals available. Open July 1 to November 1.

Hatchet Campground
Located next to Blackrock Ranger Station off Highway 287 between Moran Junction and Dubois. Nine sites. Picnic tables, drinking water and restrooms available. Open June 15 to November 1.

Atherton Creek
Located on the Gros Ventre Slide Road, accessed off the Gros Ventre Road north of Kelly. 20 sites. Picnic tables, restrooms, drinking water, boat launch, fishing and swimming available. Open June 5 to October 30.

Red Hills
Located on the Gros Ventre Slide Road, accessed off the Gros Ventre Road north of Kelly. Five sites. Picnic tables, restrooms, drinking water and fishing available. Open June 5 to October 30.

Crystal Creek
Located on the Gros Ventre Slide Road, access off the Gros Ventre Road north of Kelly. Six sites. Picnic tables, restrooms, drinking water and fishing available. Open June 5 to October 30.

Curtis Canyon
Located off Flat Creek Road, accessed through the National Elk Refuge. Road begins at the end of East Broadway in Jackson. 12 sites. Picnic tables and restrooms available. No drinking water. Open June 15 through September 19.

Granite Creek
Located on Granite Creek Road, accessed off Highway 189/91 between Hoback Junction and Bondurant. 52 sites. Picnic tables, restrooms, drinking water, and fishing available. Open June 15 to September 15.

Hoback
Located off Highway 189/91 between Hoback Junction and Bondurant. 26 sites. Picnic tables, restrooms, drinking water and fishing available. Open June 1 to September 30.

Kozy Campground
Located off Highway 189/91 between Hoback Junction and Bondurant. Eight sites. Picnic tables, restrooms and fishing available. No drinking water. Open June 1 to September 30.

Bridge
Located on Greys River Road, accessed off Highway 26/89 near Alpine. Five sites. Picnic tables, restrooms, fishing available. No drinking water. Open June 1 to September 10.

Lynx Creek
Located on Greys River Road, accessed off Highway 26/89 near Alpine. 14 sites. Picnic tables, restrooms, fishing available. No drinking water. Open June 15 to September 10.

Murphy Creek
Located on Greys River Road, accessed off Highway 26/89 near Alpine. 10 sites. Picnic tables, restrooms, fishing available. No drinking water. Open June 15 to September 10.

TARGHEE CAMPGROUNDS ADMINISTERED BY BTNF
All of the campgrounds below are located off of U.S. Highway 26/89 between Hoback and Alpine junctions.

Cabin Creek
10 Sites. Picnic tables, restrooms, drinking water and fishing available. Open May 25 to September 5.

East Elbow
Nine sites. Picnic tables, restrooms, drinking water, boat launch and fishing available. Open May 25 to September 5.
West Elbow
Eight sites. Picnic tables, restrooms, drinking water, fishing, group reservations available. Open May 25 to September 5.
East Table Creek
18 sites. Picnic tables, restrooms, drinking water, boat launch and fishing available. Open May 25 to September 5.
Station Creek
14 sites. Picnic tables, restrooms, drinking water and fishing available. Open May 25 to September 5.
Wolf Creek
10 sites. Picnic tables, restrooms and fishing available. No drinking water. Open May 25 to September 5.

BTNF/TARGHEE GUIDED HIKES
The Hole Hiking Experience
The Hole Hiking Experience offers guided hikes on Bridger-Teton and parts of Targhee National Forest. Half, full, and multi-day, naturalist-led trips are offered. For information and reservations, call 307-739-7155.

TARGHEE NATIONAL FOREST

PHONE NUMBERS
Emergencies 911
Supervisor's Office 208-624-3151
Forest Conditions (recorded) 208-624-4576
   Weekends and evenings

OFFICES
Supervisors Office 208-624-3151
P.O. Box 208
St. Anthony, Idaho 83445
Dubois Ranger District 208-374-5422
Dubois, Idaho 83423
Teton Basin District 208-354-2312
Driggs, Idaho 83422

Island Park Ranger District 208-558-7301
Island Park, Idaho 83429
Ashton Ranger District 208-652-7442
Ashton, Idaho 83420
Palisades Ranger District 208-523-1412
P.O. Box 398B Route 1
Idaho Falls, Idaho 83401

CAMPING
Fees for camping are based on facilities provided in the campground. Most undeveloped areas within the forest are open to camping. Stay limit is posted at each campground. Since some areas do not have garbage service, you need to bring your own refuse bags.

Teton Canyon
Located on Teton Canyon Road, accessed off Ski Hill Road between Alta and Grand Targhee Ski area. Nine sites. Picnic tables, restrooms, drinking water, trailer sites and fishing available. Open August 1 to September 30.

Trail Creek
Located off Wyoming Hwy. 22 between Wilson, Wyoming and Victor, Idaho. 11 sites. Restrooms, drinking water, trailer parking and fishing available. Open June 1 to September 30.

Mike Harris
Located off Idaho Hwy. 33 between Wilson, Wyoming and Victor, Idaho. 12 sites. Restrooms, drinking water, trailer parking and fishing available. Open June 1 to September 30.

OFF-ROAD VEHICLES
A majority of Targhee National Forest is open to off-road vehicle use. To protect natural resources such as soils, water and wildlife, OVR use is restricted in certain areas. Free Forest Travel Plan maps showing these areas are available at Forest Service offices

INDEX

▲

A

Absaroka Range 123, 130
Aerial tram 97
Alaska Basin 41, 44, 75, 76
Alder Creek 163
Amoretti, Eugene 127
Amphitheater Lake 23, 33
Andy Stone Trail 80
Angles Entrance 114
Ann's Ridge 163
Antoinette Peak 142
Apres Vous Peak 97
Arizona Creek 119
Arizona Creek Trail 119
Arrowhead Pool 47
Astorians 157
Avalanche Canyon 22, 25
Avalanche Canyon Divide 44

B

Bailey Meadows 119
Baldy Knoll 71
Basin Creek Meadows 129
Basin Lakes 62, 75
Battleship Mountain 75, 76
Bear Canyon 69
Bear Cub Pass 127
Bear River Range 158
Bearpaw Bay 38
Bearpaw Lake 38
Beaver Mountain 160
Betty Davis' Eyes 138
Big Piney Ranger District 158
Binkle, William 122
Black Canyon 86
Black Canyon Creek 86
Blackrock Creek 116

Blind Canyon 171
Blue Miner Lake 137
Bondurant 162
Bondurant Creek 166
Bonneville Creek 126
Bonneville Pass 128
Bonneville Pass Trail 127
Box Creek Canyon 109
Box Creek Trailhead 109, 112
Bradley, Frank 23
Bradley Lake 22
Brooks Lake 126, 128
Brooks Lake Campground 126, 128
Brooks Lake Creek 128
Brooks Lake Lodge 126, 128
Brown's Meadows 120
Bryan Flats Guard Station 164
Buck Mountain 19, 21
Buffalo Ranger District 108
Buffalo River Valley 110
Buffalo Valley Road 109
Bunker Creek 142
Burbank Creek 90

C

Cabin Creek 168
Cabin Creek Trail 168
Cache Creek 151
Cache Creek Canyon 150, 151
Cache Creek Pass 142
Cache Creek Trail 142
Camp Davis 163
Carnes, John 149
Cascade Canyon 37, 40
Cascade Creek 42
Casper Bowl 97
Cathedral Group 37
CCC 34, 122, 144
Chief Joseph 65
Christian Pond 56

Clark's Draw 162
Clause Peak 163
Cleaver Peak 81
Clendenning Lake 129
Cliff Creek 166
Cliff Creek Canyon 166
Cliff Creek Falls 165
Cliff Creek Road 166
Climber's Ranch 27
Coal Creek 67
Coal Creek Canyon 61
Cody Bowl 100
Cody Bowl Lake 100
Colter Bay 52
Cottonwood Creek 26
Cow Creek 159
Cow Creek Trail 159
Crater Lake 86
Cream Puff Peak 159
Crystal Creek 138
Cub Creek 115
Cube Point 46
Curtis Canyon 153
Curtis Canyon Campground 153
Cygnet Pond 56

D

Danford, Marion 102
Darby Canyon 72
Darby Creek 72
Darby Formation 72
Dartmouth Basin 30
Davis, Eleanor 28
Deadhorse Peak 171
Death Canyon 19
Death Canyon Patrol Cabin 19
Death Canyon Shelf 61
Delta Lake 35
Detweiler, Mike 149
Devil's Stairs 75
Disappointment Peak 34

Divide Creek Trail 113
Dog Creek 170
Dog-Faced Pete 120
Don, Dr. MacLeod 140
Doubletop Peak 140, 146
Dry Fork Canyon 171
Dundee Creek 129
DuNoir Trail 128

E

Eagle Peak 140
East Table Trail 170
Elk Mountain 173
Elk tuskers 122
Elkhorn Store 146
Ellingwood, Albert 28
Emma Matilda Lake 58
Enos, John 113
Enos Lake 112, 113

F

Flat Creek 154
Flat Creek Divide 144
Flat Creek Trail 144
Forks of Cascade Canyon 42
Fort Astoria 157
Fossil Mountain 62, 71
Fox Creek Canyon 71, 77
Fox Creek Pass 20, 102
Fred's Mountain 78

G

Game Creek 151, 154
Game Creek Canyon 70
Game Creek Divide 71
Game Creek Divide 102
Game Creek Road 151
Garnet Canyon 29
Garnet Creek 29
Geraldine Lucas Rock 26

Gin Pole Draw 151
Glacier Gulch 33
Glacier Trail 33
Glory Bowl 84
Glory Slide 86
Goodwin Lake 152
Grand Teton 10, 17, 79
Grand Teton National Park 17
Granite Basin 81
Granite Canyon 104
Granite Canyon Patrol Cabin 105
Granite Creek 105
Granite Creek Campground 140
Granite Hot Springs 140, 144
Granite Ranch 140
Granite Recreation Area 140
Gravel Mountain 113
Gravel Ridge 113
Green Lake 81
Green Lakes 80
Green Mountain 80
Greys River Road 173
Grizzly Bear Lake 50
Gros Ventre 131, 139
Gros Ventre Peak 142, 144
Gros Ventre Range 140
Gros Ventre River 139
Gros Ventre Slide 135

H

Hanging Canyon 46
Hanging Canyon Creek 47
Hayden Expedition 78
Hermitage Point 52
Heron Pond 52
Hidden Falls 37, 42
Hoback Canyon 157, 166

Hoback Guard Station 163
Hoback, John 123, 157
Hoback Peak 158
Hoback River Canyon 157
Hodges Peak 140
Holland, John 149
Holly Lake 48, 63
Holmes Cave 116
Honeymoon Lake Trail 166
House Creek 146
Housetop Mountain 70, 101
Huckleberry Lookout 122
Huckleberry Mountain 120, 121
Huckleberry Ridge 122
Hunt's Pass 157
Hurricane Pass 41, 44, 77

I

Ice Cave 72
Inspiration Point 42
Isabel, Charles 122

J

Jackson 149
Jackson, Davey 9
Jackson District 132
Jackson Hole 9, 149
Jackson Hole Coal Company 131
Jackson Lake 52, 58
Jackson Lake Lodge 55
Jackson Peak 152
Jackson Ranger District 150
Jackson, William 44, 78
Jacob, John Astor 157
Jade Lake 125
Jedediah Smith Wilderness 65
Jenny Lake 36
Jules Bowl 128

JY Ranch 20

K

Karst topography 100
Kelly 135
Kisinger Lake 128
Kisinger Lakes Trail 128
Kitten Ridge 119

L

Lafayette Guard Station 165
Lake of the Crags 46
Lake Solitude 41, 63
Lake Taminah 26
Lakeshore Trail 53
Laurel Lake 38
Lava Creek Trail 110
Leek, Holly 50
Leek, Stephen 50
Leeks Canyon 155
Leigh Canyon 37
Leigh Lake 36
Little Greys River 173
Little Jenny Ranch 146
Little Red Creek 171
Littles Peak 44
Lone Eagle 165
Lookouts 173
Lower Brooks Lake 126
Lower Jade Lake 125
Lower Saddle 30
Lower Slide Lake 135
Lucas, Geraldine 27
Lucas Ranch 27
Lupine Meadows 29, 33

M

MacLeod Lake 140

Maidenform Peak 81
Mail Cabin Canyon 88
Mail Cabin Canyon Trail 94
Mail Cabin Creek 91, 94
Marion Lake 62, 71, 104
McCollister, Paul 97
Mesquite Creek Divide, 67
Mesquite Pass 62
Middle Fork Cutoff Trail 62, 105
Middle Ridge 173
Middle Teton 29
Mike Harris Campground 69, 92
Mike Harris Trail 92
Mikesell Canyon 90
Miller Draw 162
Monument Ridge 162
Moose Canyon 70
Moose Creek 69
Moose Creek Divide 61, 104
Moose Lake 70, 103
Moose Pond Overlook 37
Moosehead Ranch 133
Moran Bay 38
Mosquito Creek 88
Mount Bannon 62
Mount Glory 84
Mount Hunt 71
Mount Jedediah Smith 62
Mount Meek 62, 76
Mount Meek Pass 62, 76, 77
Mount Moran 37
Mount Owen 35
Mount St. John 38, 47
Mount Woodring 48
Mt. Alpenglow 21
Mt. Leidy 112, 134
Mt. Owen 42

Munger Mountain 167
Mystic Isle 38

N

National Elk Refuge 154
Noker, John 152
Noker Mine Draw 152
Nordwall Campground 68, 69
North Fork of the Palisades 90
North Fork Trail 102
Nowlin Meadows 115

O

Off-trail travel 13
Old Man Flats 154
Old Pass Road 86
Oliver Peak 92
Open Canyon 20
Open Door Pinnacle 140
Oregon Short Line Railroad 83
Owen, William 30
Owen-Spalding Route 28
Oxbow Bend 59

P

Pacific Creek 112
Pacific Fur Company 157
Paintbrush Canyon 38, 44, 48
Paintbrush Divide 18, 44, 61
Palisades Reservoir 146
Palmer Peak 149
Panorama House 163
Parody Draw 154
Peak 9,279 86
Peak 9,301 170
Perch's Pond 42
Petzoldt, Paul 45
Petzoldt's Caves 30
Phelps Lake 20
Phelps Lake Overlook 19

Phillips Canyon 68
Phillips Canyon Road 87
Phillips Pass 61
Pika 100
Pilgrim Creek 55
Pilgrim Creek Trail 120
Pilot Knobs 9
Pinnacle Butte 128, 129
Pinnacle Peak 160
Pinnacle Trail 135
Pinnacles 124, 129
Plummer Canyon 71
Pole Canyon 96
Price, William Hunt 157
Purdy, Charles 122
Pyramid Peak 142

R

Rainbow Lake 126
Ramshead Lake 47
Ramshead Trail 176
Ramshorn Peak 141, 163
Red Creek 171
Red Hills 139
Red Hills Campground 137
Red Hills Ranch 139
Red Peak 171
Rendezvous Peak 69, 97, 101
Ribbon Cascades 47
Richards, Homer 34
Ridgetop Trail 85
Roaring Creek 76
Rock Creek 146
Rock of Ages 47
Rock Springs Bowl 99
Rockchuck Peak 38, 48
Rodent Creek 122

S

Salt River Range 184

Sandy Marshall Creek 166
Schoolroom Glacier 45
Schwabacher's Landing 51
Scott, Gibb 34
Second Creek 56
Sheep Creek Road 153
Sheep Mountain 137, 153
Sheffield Creek Trail 121
Shoal Falls 140
Shoal Lake 141
Shoal Lake Trail 140
Shoshoko Falls 25
Shoshone National Forest 127
Simpson Peak 118
Ski Lake 87
Sleeping Indian 138
Snag Creek 166
Snake River 85
Snake River Canyon 173
Snake River Land Company 28
Snake River Range 85
Snow King 154
Snow King Ski Area 154
Snowdrift Lake 26
Soda Fork Trail 115
Sourdough Creek 175
South Buffalo Fork 114
South Buffalo Fork Gorge 115
South Fork Falls 114
South Fork of Cascade Canyon 62, 77
South Leigh Creek 44
South Teton Canyon 75
South Teton Creek 76
Spalding Falls 30
Spalding, Frank 30
Spearhead Peak 71
Static Peak 19, 21
Static Peak Divide 18, 19
Storm Point 42

193

String Lake 36, 37
Sublette, William 9
Surprise Lake 34
Swan Lake 52
Swift Creek Trailhead 140

T

Table Mountain 44, 79
Taggart Lake 22, 25
Taggart, W.R. 23
Targhee 65
Targhee National Forest 65
Taylor Mountain 67
Teewinot 42
Terrace Meadows 115
Terrace Mountain 115
Teton Canyon Shelf 75, 76
Teton Crest Trail 61, 70, 76, 104
Teton Pass 83, 157
Teton Village 95
Teton Wilderness 107
The Meadows 29
The Wall 44, 75
Third Creek 53
Tin Cup Creek 80
Togwotee 123
Togwotee Pass 123
Togwotee Lodge 114
Toppings, Fred 133
Toppings Lakes 133
Tornado 109
Tosi Peak 140
Town Square 150
Trail Creek 173
Trapper Lake 38
Triangle Peak 140
Turquoise Lake 142
Two Ocean Lake 59

U

Upper Brooks Lake 125
Upper Jade Lake 125

V

Valhalla Canyon 42
Valley Trail 20

W

Waterfall Canyon 54
Weather 14
West Dell Creek 146
West Dell Creek Falls 144
West DuNoir Creek 129
West Gros Ventre Butte 154
West Miner Creek 138
West Shoal Creek 141
Wildcat Peak 120
William, Capt. A. Jones 123
Willow Creek 163
Willow Creek Trail 163
Willow Flats 55
Wilson Canyon 155
Wind Cave 72
Wind River Ranger District 124
Wolf Mountain 168
Wyoming Peak 158
Wyoming Range 162

Y

Younts Peak 107

TREK THE HIMALAYAS

NEPAL
Ama Dablam and Tengboche Monastery

If you like to hike, you'll love trekking in Nepal. The Kingdom of Nepal is a narrow sliver of land squeezed between burgeoning India to the south and the vast Tibetan plateau to the north. She rises from plain to plain, valley to valley, mountain to mountain — a precipitous staircase that ends at the roof of the world: The Himalayas, "abode of the snows." Eight of the world's 10 highest summits lie within her borders.

For her size and population, Nepal is the least roaded country in the world. To see her, you must travel as her people do — on foot. EcoVentures can get you there. The culturally and environmentally sensitive travel company is owned by Becky Woods and Rich Bloom, a married team who collectively have guided people throughout the world for over 30 years.

Becky has traveled extensively through the Himalayas since the 1980s, leading trips to every corner of Nepal. She speaks Nepali and is well-versed of the country's diverse culture and religions. When not guiding in Nepal or Tibet, she writes. She is the author of this guidebook and *Walking the Winds*, a guide to Wyoming's Wind River Range.

Rich Bloom has guided in Nepal, United States, Canada, Mexico, Chile, and Patagonia through EcoVentures and pioneer outdoor organizations such as the National Outdoor Leadership School (NOLS) and Colorado Outward Bound. He is an accomplished mountaineer, sea kayaker and whitewater boater as well as a naturalist who has worked with numerous field science schools. When not guiding, Rich works as an environmental education consultant.

Becky and Rich work with a fine Sherpa staff, many of them veterans of Everest and other 8,000 meter Himalayan expeditions. Their staff prepares meals and carries out all camp duties. Porters and pack animals carry gear. You have only to carry a daypack large enough for a water bottle, a camera and an extra jacket. It is a wonderful way to travel through the highest mountains in the world.

For additional information, or to be placed on EcoVentures mailing list, please fill in the coupon on the following page.

YES.

I WANT MORE INFORMATION ON VISITING THE HIMALAYAS. PUT ME ON YOUR MAILING LIST.

NAME_____
ADDRESS_____
CITY/STATE/ZIP_____
PHONE_____

EcoVentures
Box 623
Wilson, Wyoming 83014
mountains@wyoming.com

Order Form

To order additional copies of this book, please check your local bookstore/outdoor shop. If not available, send a check or money order to: White Willow Publishing, Star Route 3272, Jackson, Wyoming, 83001, in the amount of $14.95 plus $1.50 for shipping and handling for each copy. Please fill in the information below:

NAME_____

ADDRESS_____

CITY/STATE/ZIP_____

Walking the Winds: A Hiking and Fishing Guide to Wyoming's Wind River Range by the same author is also available from White Willow Publishing. Please send $12.95 plus $1.50 for shipping for each copy ordered.

White Willow Publishing
Star Route 3272 • Jackson, Wyoming 83001
307-733-0674 • rbloom@wyoming.com

Wholesale/Dealer inquiries invited